THE QUILT
ENGAGEMENT CALENDAR
TREASURY

THE QUILT ENGAGEMENT

CYRIL I. NELSON
&
CARTER HOUCK

CALENDAR TREASURY

Including complete patterns and instructions for making your own quilts

E. P. DUTTON, INC.
New York

1. Pieced quilt, Medallion, designed and made by Sherry Phillips, 1979, Brimson, Minnesota. 100″ x 90″. Using an adaptation of the traditional Pineapple block, the artist has created a particularly beautiful quilt aglow with Fall colors. This piece was displayed and sold at the Quilt National '79 in Athens, Ohio. Photograph by Sherry Phillips courtesy Bonnie Leman, editor, *Quilter's Newsletter Magazine*. (Private collection)

Other examples of Medallion quilts are illustrated in plates 2, 3, 4, 13, 35, 36, 45, 49, 51, 54, 55, 57, 58, 70, 82, 83, 84, 99, 102, 106, 107, 108, 119, 122, 127, 128, 138, 146, 159, 164, 175, 176, 183.

Pages ii–iii: Installation view from the exhibition, "Baltimore Album Quilts," curated by Dena S. Katzenberg at The Baltimore Museum of Art, Baltimore, Maryland, December 13, 1981–February 7, 1982. Photograph courtesy The Baltimore Museum of Art.

Pages vi, vii, and 4: Details from an Album/Medallion quilt, c. 1845, possibly Pennsylvania. See plate 4 for an illustration of the complete quilt.

2. Pieced quilt, Medallion, 1850–1860. 34″ x 33¼″. Although it is possible that this jaunty piece was intended to be a crib quilt, it seems more likely that it began life as the center of a Medallion quilt that was never finished or that lost its borders along the way. Never mind; it will bloom forever! Photograph courtesy Thos. K. Woodard: American Antiques & Quilts. (Private collection)

Other examples of Medallion quilts are illustrated in plates 1, 3, 4, 13, 35, 36, 45, 49, 51, 54, 55, 57, 58, 70, 82, 83, 84, 99, 102, 106, 107, 108, 119, 122, 127, 128, 138, 146, 159, 164, 175, 176, 183.

ACKNOWLEDGMENTS

Grateful thanks are due to the many collectors, dealers, and museums whose interest and gracious cooperation have made this book possible: Adirondack Memories, Glens Falls, New York; M. J. Albacete, The Canton Art Institute, Canton, Ohio; America Hurrah Antiques, N.Y.C.; Leonard and Jackie Balish; Teresa Barkley; Darwin D. Bearley, Akron, Ohio; The Brick Store Museum, Kennebunk, Maine; Gary Brockman; Abby Brooks; Dorothy Brooks; Gary C. Cole, New York; The Connecticut Historical Society, Hartford, Connecticut; Nancy Crow, Baltimore, Ohio; Sharon D'Atri, The Canton Art Institute, Canton, Ohio; David Davies; Historic Deerfield, Inc., Deerfield, Massachusetts; Frederick Di Maio: Inglenook Antiques, New York; Bill Gallick and Tony Ellis; Cora Ginsburg, Benjamin Ginsburg—Antiquary, New York; Guido Goldman; Rhea Goodman, New York; Phyllis Haders, New York; Bryce and Donna Hamilton, Minneapolis, Minnesota; Barbara S. Janos, New York; Margot Strand Jensen, Aurora, Colorado; Jay Johnson: America's Folk Heritage Gallery, New York; Alice Kaplan; Dena S. Katzenberg, The Baltimore Museum of Art, Baltimore, Maryland; Kelter-Malcé Antiques, New York; Kiracofe and Kile, San Francisco, California; Malcolm Kirk; John Klassen, The Massillon Museum, Massillon, Ohio; Kornblee Gallery, New York; Edward Larson, Chicago, Illinois; Bonnie Leman, *Quilter's Newsletter Magazine*, Wheatridge, Colorado; Mr. and Mrs. Paul Martinson; James Mincemoyer; Bettie Mintz: All of Us Americans Folk Art, Bethesda, Maryland; Montclair Crafters Guild, Montclair, New Jersey; Museum of American Folk Art, New York; New Canaan Bank and Trust Company, New Canaan, Connecticut; Sherry Phillips; Nancy Boyle Press, The Baltimore Museum of Art, Baltimore, Maryland; Jane Reeves, The Canton Art Institute, Canton, Ohio; Linda Reuther; George E. Schoellkopf Gallery, New York; Jacqueline Schuman; Julie Silber; Fran Soika, Novelty, Ohio; Sotheby Parke Bernet, Inc., New York; Betty Sterling, New York; Lois Stulberg; Phyllis Varineau; Wild Goose Chase Quilt Gallery, Evanston, Illinois; The Henry Francis du Pont Winterthur Museum, Winterthur, Delaware; and Thos. K. Woodard: American Antiques & Quilts, New York.

CONTENTS

3. Appliqué quilt, Medallion/Broderie Perse, c. 1830, Paducah, Kentucky. 120" x 122". This masterpiece of design and needlework must be studied with a magnifying glass so that one may fully appreciate the infinite care and delicacy with which the chintz cutouts and the stuffed work in the background have been created and combined in this incredible quilt. Photograph courtesy America Hurrah Antiques, N.Y.C. (Private collection)

Other examples of Broderie Perse quilts are illustrated in plates 99, 128, 130, 145.

Other examples of quilts with stuffed work are illustrated in plates 10, 12, 58, 74, 99, 100, 146, 180.

Other examples of Medallion quilts are illustrated in plates 1, 2, 4, 13, 35, 36, 45, 49, 51, 54, 55, 57, 58, 70, 82, 83, 84, 99, 102, 106, 107, 108, 119, 122, 127, 128, 138, 146, 159, 164, 175, 176, 183.

"LOOK WHAT *I* DID!"

Pride, delight, and exultation are intermixed in that exclamation—words that must have been spoken or at least felt by each of the artists whose quilts have been collected in this treasury. The actual words are, however, spoken by Christine Miller in Pat Ferrero's fine documentary film, *Quilts in Women's Lives*, in that moving section in which Christine and her sister Hortense describe their joy in making quilts.

This sense of deep joy and pride in their artistry and accomplishment certainly has been an underlying theme of the quilt exhibitions that have been held in recent years. First, of course, was the great eye-opener in 1971 at the Whitney Museum of American Art in New York City, July 1–September 12, 1971, "Abstract Design in American Quilts," based on the extraordinary collection belonging to Jonathan Holstein and Gail van der Hoof. Three noteworthy recent shows were: "American Quilts—A Handmade Legacy," curated in 1981 by Linda Reuther and Julie Silber at the Oakland Museum, Oakland, California; "Baltimore Album Quilts," curated by Dena S. Katzenberg and shown at The Museum of Fine Arts, Houston, Texas, at The Metropolitan Museum of Art, New York City, and at The Baltimore Museum of Art in Maryland between November 1980 and February 1982; and "Ohio Quilts: A Living Tradition," curated by M. J. Albacete, Sharon D'Atri, and Jane Reeves at The Canton Art Institute, Canton, Ohio, in 1982. On pages ii–iii of this book is an installation view from the Baltimore show; a similar photograph from the Canton exhibition is on pages 2–3.

The quilt as a work of art is, of course, what *The Quilt Engagement Calendar* has been all about since its first edition in 1975. Now, eight years later, seemed a good time at which to collect together some of the best quilts illustrated in the calendar—particularly since many devotees have written to request copies of earlier issues of the calendar. Hence this treasury containing 185 quilts in color, most of which were reproduced in the eight calendars between 1975 and 1982, but a few new quilts have also crept into the collection because each has a special appeal. As such a large group of quilts is being illustrated, it seemed a good idea to provide an informal system of cross-references to the various main types of quilts that one can find in the book, such as Amish Center Diamond, Broderie Perse, Feathered Star, Log Cabin, Medallion, Pot of Flowers, and so forth. These cross-references, which are given under each of the pertinent captions, enable you to make your own comparisons and contrasts within a given type of quilt, and they become an index to the extraordinary wealth of imagination and creativity represented here.

Because fine quilts should prove an inspiration to those with the skills to make them it seemed appropriate to include at the end of this volume patterns and instructions for twenty-one quilts, each of which is based on one of the color plates. Carter Houck, author of *American Quilts and How to Make Them* (1975) and editor of the quarterly magazine *Lady's Circle Patchwork Quilts*, has graciously joined me in this venture by creating the patterns section, which is enhanced by Marilyn Rey's exquisite line drawings.

1

Installation view from the exhibition, "Ohio Quilts: A Living Tradition," curated by M. J. Albacete, Sharon D'Atri, and Jane Reeves at The Canton Art Institute, Canton, Ohio, January 28–March 14, 1982. This photograph shows a group of seven Amish quilts made in Ohio from the collection of Darwin D. Bearley, Akron, Ohio. The eighth quilt (third from the left) is a contemporary piece by Terrie Hancock Mangat called *Covington Slickers: Rainy Days in Cincinnati,* © 1981. Photograph courtesy The Canton Art Institute.

Other examples of Midwestern Amish quilts are illustrated in plates 5, 23, 62, 172.

In presenting the quilt calendar each year I have hoped that the quilts would brighten the weeks they illustrate. Because there are so many quilts in this book it is probably more appropriate to give you my wish that they will bring much beauty, joy, and interest to your homes for years to come.

In closing, it is my privilege to quote what has been said so eloquently about quilts by the previously mentioned Linda Reuther and Julie Silber who, until recently, were the proprietors of a shop in San Rafael, California, called Mary Strickler's Quilt:

After we opened the store we traveled to different parts of the country and everywhere we went we saw how quilts join people—to their families, to their communities, to their ancestors, to hidden or forgotten aspects of themselves. We learned something we had always felt: that quilts were the embodiment of a way of life and a particular form of caring. We began talking to groups of people about this and curating shows like our exhibition last year at the Oakland Museum. We wanted to show how quilts grew out of the lives of the people who made them, and how the essential qualities of those lives—dignity, strength, warmth, and integrity—have been kept alive in the present through quilts.

CYRIL I. NELSON

4. Appliqué and pieced quilt, Album/Medallion, c. 1845, possibly Pennsylvania. 109″ x 110″. And what an Album quilt this is! Seldom does one discover a quilt that combines such a wealth of wonderfully imaginative forms with great fabrics and color. This piece is an incredible work of American decorative art demanding careful scrutiny. Details from this quilt have been enlarged and reproduced on pages vi, vii, and 4.

Other examples of Album quilts are illustrated in plates 7, 74, 80, 87, 115, 147, 174.

Other examples of Medallion quilts are illustrated in plates 1, 2, 3, 13, 35, 36, 45, 49, 51, 54, 55, 57, 58, 70, 82, 83, 84, 99, 102, 106, 107, 108, 119, 122, 127, 128, 138, 146, 159, 164, 175, 176, 183.

5. Appliqué quilt, Stars and Leaves, Amish, c. 1920, Ohio. 86″ x 72″. The Amish in the Midwest are particularly noted for their quilts created with a dark palette. The blue and black work brilliantly together here. (Kelter-Malcé Antiques)

Other examples of Midwestern Amish quilts are illustrated on pages 2–3 and in plates 23, 41, 62, 172.

6. Pieced quilt, Center Diamond, wool, Amish, c. 1920, Lancaster County, Pennsylvania. 77″ x 77″. This handsome Center Diamond is made especially interesting by the inclusion of a square of Sunshine and Shadow design within the central diamond. (George E. Schoellkopf Gallery)

Other examples of Amish Center Diamond quilts are illustrated in plates 8, 66, 97, 124, 126, 142, 154.

7. Appliqué quilt top, Album, 1858–1863, vicinity of Poughkeepsie, New York. 87″ x 71½″. This masterpiece of American folk art is dated by the design patterns cut from contemporary newspapers that survived with the quilt. Since its publication as the frontispiece for the *Quilt Calendar* of 1975, it has become one of the most famous of American quilts—and deservedly so. Photograph courtesy George E. Schoellkopf Gallery. (Museum of American Folk Art; Gift of the Trustees)

Other examples of Album quilts are illustrated in plates 4, 74, 80, 87, 115, 147, 174.

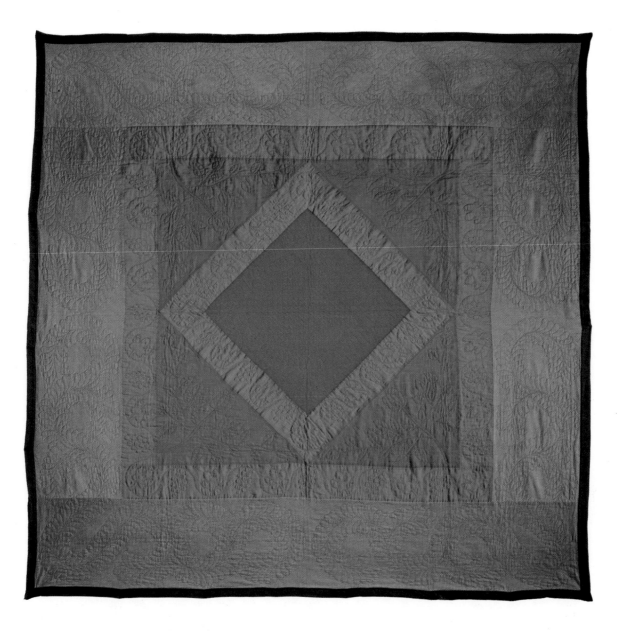

8. Pieced quilt, Center Diamond, wool, Amish, c. 1900, Lancaster County, Pennsylvania. 78″ x 78″. Many fine Amish Center diamonds have appeared since this marvel was published in the 1975 *Quilt Calendar*, but I have yet to see it surpassed in sheer breathtaking color. (Phyllis Haders)

Other examples of Amish Center Diamond quilts are illustrated in plates 6, 66, 97, 124, 126, 142, 154.

9. Pieced and appliqué quilt, Flower Basket, 1850–1860. 108″ x 84″. The serpentine sashes and borders on this quilt make it unusually exciting in its graphic quality. Photograph courtesy Leonard and Jackie Balish. (Betty Sterling)

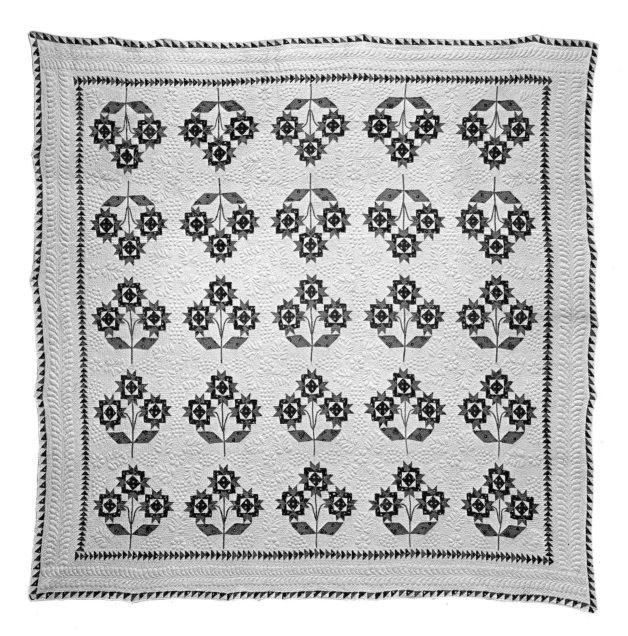

10. Pieced Flower quilt with stuffed work, c. 1850, New England. 88″ x 88″. Every element of this piece exudes delicacy and refinement; note the tiny pieces in the borders and the beauty of the stuffed work. (Phyllis Haders)

Other examples of quilts with stuffed work are illustrated in plates 3, 12, 58, 74, 99, 100, 146, 180.

11. Appliqué quilt, Stars, Leaves, and Currants, c. 1910, Ohio. 80″ x 80″. Not only is this piece beautifully designed and quilted, but it also possesses an extraordinary rhythm, almost as if the large motifs were lightheartedly swirling through a waltz. (Kelter-Malcé Antiques)

12. Appliqué quilt, Whig Rose variation, 1845–1855. 78″ x 76″. The wonderfully free and imaginative stuffed designs become the dominant motifs in this delicate quilt. (America Hurrah Antiques, N.Y.C.)

Other examples of quilts with stuffed work are illustrated in plates 3, 10, 58, 74, 99, 100, 146, 180.

13. Bed rug, Medallion, signed and dated "Mary Foot AD 1778," wool sewn in running and pattern darning stitches on a natural wool foundation, probably Colchester, Connecticut, area. 77″ x 77½″. Bed rugs are the rarest type of American bedcovers, as well as being among the handsomest. Most date to the late eighteenth or early nineteenth century. Note the variety of patterns created by the stitches. (The Henry Francis du Pont Winterthur Museum)

Other examples of Medallion quilts are illustrated in plates 1, 2, 3, 4, 35, 36, 45, 49, 51, 54, 55, 57, 58, 70, 82, 83, 84, 99, 102, 106, 107, 108, 119, 122, 127, 128, 138, 146, 159, 164, 175, 176, 183.

14. Pieced quilt, Houses and Barns, c. 1910, Massachusetts. 88″ x 84″. First published in the 1975 *Quilt Calendar*, this is still one of the most complex and satisfying examples of House quilts. Photograph courtesy Phyllis Haders. (Thos. K. Woodard: American Antiques & Quilts)

Other examples of House quilts are illustrated in plates 34, 46, 140.

15. Pieced quilt, Pot of Flowers, wool embroidered with polychrome wools in crewel stitches, c. 1830, probably New England. 117″ x 92″. The Pot of Flowers motif is one of the most popular in American quilts. Here the embroidered floral motifs are beautifully highlighted by the blue and brown background. (The Henry Francis du Pont Winterthur Museum)

Other examples of Pot of Flowers quilts are illustrated in plates 20, 21, 60, 149, 157, 173, 181.

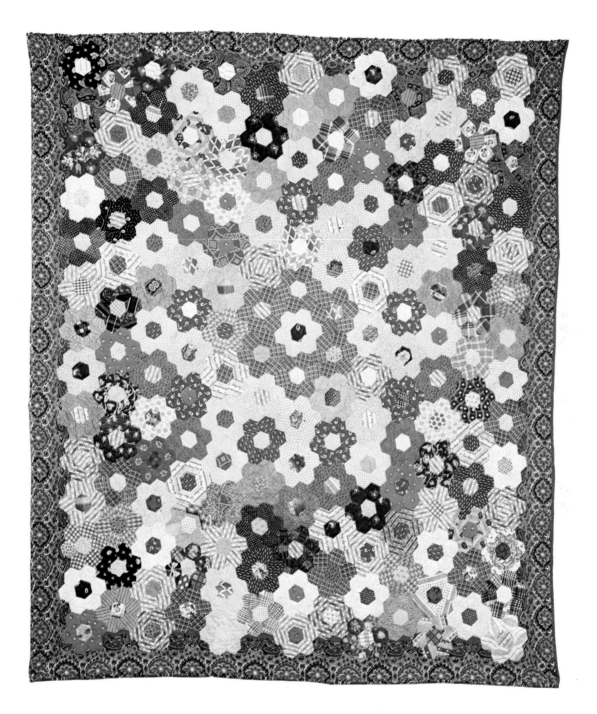

16. Pieced crib quilt, Mosaic, c. 1860, Pennsylvania. 48½″ x 39¾″. The small mosaics make up large mosaics, and they all add up to a happy, dazzling splash of color. (America Hurrah Antiques, N.Y.C.)

Other examples of crib quilts are illustrated in plates 28, 65, 75, 111, 150, 165.

17. Pieced presentation quilt, Johnny 'Round the Corner, dated 1847, Montgomery County, Pennsylvania. Each of the white squares in this quilt is inscribed "Tribute of Respect 1847," and each is signed by a different person. Photograph courtesy America Hurrah Antiques, N.Y.C. (Private collection)

18. Pieced quilt, made by Maria Cadman Hubbard, dated 1848, probably New England. 88½″ x 81½″. So far as is known, this "Pieties Quilt" is a unique conception in American quilts. The individual letters are constructed of tiny bits of material pieced together. Photograph courtesy George E. Schoellkopf Gallery. (Private collection)

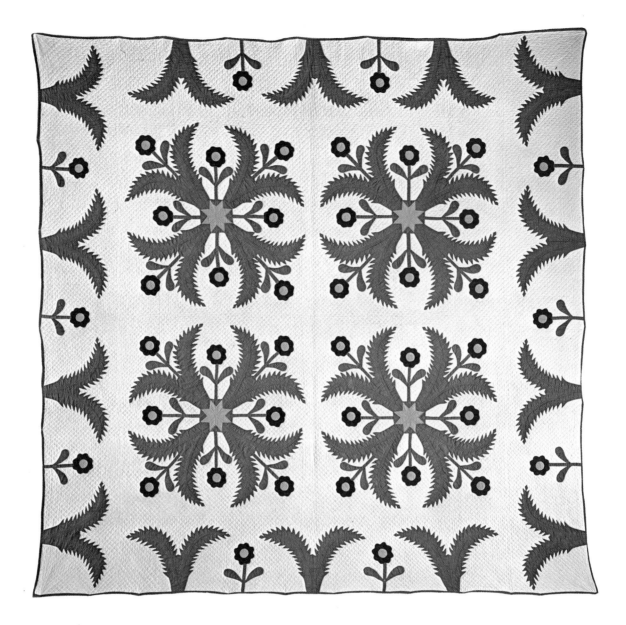

19. Appliqué quilt, Flowering Fern, c. 1880, Ohio. 92″ x 91″. The design and colors of this lovely quilt all combine to make it a celebration of the beauty and vitality of growing things. (Kelter-Malcé Antiques)

20. Pieced and appliqué quilt, Star of Bethlehem, 1880–1890, Pennsylvania. 90″ x 89″. The appealing spontaneity of good folk art is evident in this delightful piece. Note the hearts that double as blossoms in two of the Pot of Flowers motifs in the corners. (Kelter-Malcé Antiques)

Other examples of Star quilts are illustrated in plates 22, 78, 79, 85, 106, 116, 118, 129, 134, 143, 144, 152, 165, 170, 171, 178, 179, 185.

Other examples of Pot of Flowers quilts are illustrated in plates 15, 21, 60, 149, 157, 173, 181.

21. Pieced and appliqué quilt, Pot of Flowers, c. 1930. made by Mrs. C. O. Stotts, Yates County, Kansas. 96″ x 80″. The blooms in these pots provide a good sampling of typical 1930s fabrics. The impact of the quilt is enhanced by the fine quilting in the background of each of the large squares. Photograph courtesy America Hurrah Antiques, N.Y.C. (Private collection)

Other examples of Pot of Flowers quilts are illustrated in plates 15, 20, 60, 149, 157, 173, 181.

22. Pieced quilt, Star, Mennonite, made by Amy Bucher, c. 1889, Lebanon County, Pennsylvania. 83¾″ x 79¾″. Created from scraps of material left over from the making of two Lone Star quilts, this piece has a brilliant, abstract, kaleidoscopic effect. (Thos. K. Woodard: American Antiques & Quilts)

Other examples of Star quilts are illustrated in plates 20, 78, 79, 85, 106, 116, 118, 129, 134, 143, 144, 152, 165, 170, 171, 178, 179, 185.

23. Pieced quilt, Cross-in-the-Square, wool, Amish, c. 1900, Indiana. 87″ x 69″. Here is a vibrant palette of bright and dark colors expertly composed into an immensely satisfying whole, and with feather quilting adding special weight and interest to the broad sashes. (Bryce and Donna Hamilton)

Other examples of Midwestern Amish quilts are illustrated on pages 2–3 and in plates 5, 41, 62, 172.

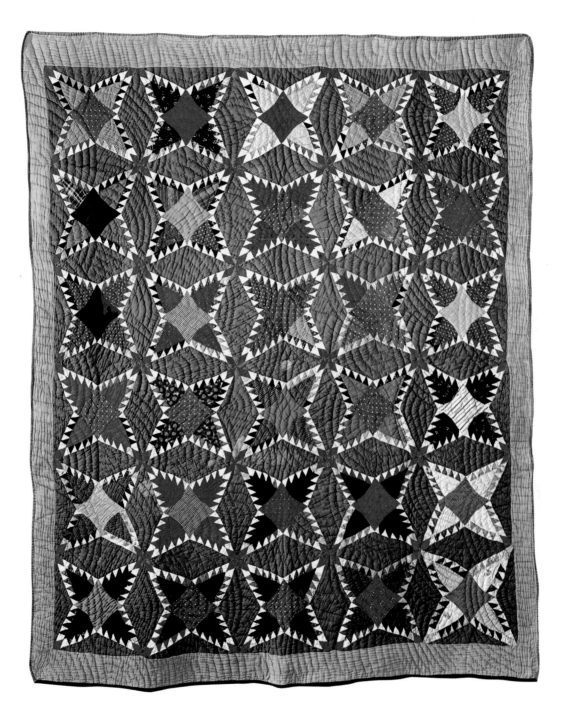

24. Pieced quilt, Feathered World Without End, c. 1900, Pennsylvania. 84″ x 66″. Unusual colors, bold graphics, and a warm, heavy texture make this a splendid country quilt. (Kelter-Malcé Antiques)

25. Pieced quilt, Log Cabin, Windmill Blades or Pineapple design, c. 1900, Pennsylvania. First published in the 1977 calendar, the color and energy of this piece make it still one of the most powerful Pineapple Log Cabins I have seen. (Bryce and Donna Hamilton)

Other examples of Log Cabin quilts are illustrated in plates 32, 52, 61, 63, 69, 90, 94, 112, 123, 125, 131, 167.

26. Pieced and embroidered quilt, Crazy, c. 1890, New Jersey. 70″ x 70″. The rich fabrics, handsome designs, and extraordinarily fine embroidery make this a superlative example of a Victorian Crazy quilt, worthy of a museum. It is inscribed "S. J. Buell" on the red pennant at the top of the left mast of the sailboat. Photograph courtesy George E. Schoellkopf Gallery. (Mary Strickler's Quilt)

Other examples of Crazy quilts are illustrated in plates 31, 73, 89, 93, 140.

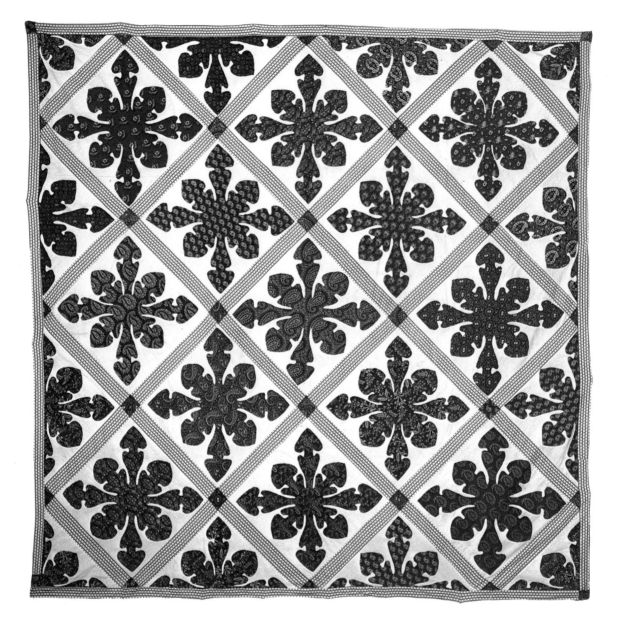

27. Pieced and appliqué quilt, Double Hearts, 1850–1860. 94″ x 92″. Strikingly organized by the blue diagonals, the appliquéd motifs in this quilt comprise a rich collection of patterns, mostly of the Paisley type. (Jay Johnson: America's Folk Heritage Gallery)

28. Appliqué crib quilt, c. 1860, New York State. 38″ x 38″. The bold forms used in this charming miniature seem to mirror the chubbiness of the babe for whom the quilt was made. (Phyllis Haders)

Other examples of crib quilts are illustrated in plates 16, 65, 75, 111, 150, 165.

29. Appliqué quilt, c. 1855, Vermont. 90″ x 83″. This floral design has been exceptionally well designed and crafted. The piece is quite formally constructed in terms of symmetrical balance, yet the designs also flow with a sense of natural grace, enhanced by the rhythm of the serpentine border. The bits of bright yellow spotted throughout also give an airy touch to the whole. Compare the leaf quilt in plate 35 where a roughly similar design ripples with life. Photograph courtesy Thos. K. Woodard: American Antiques & Quilts. (Private collection)

30. Pieced and appliqué quilt, 1976, Montclair, New Jersey. 84″ x 72″. Made by thirty needlewomen of the Montclair Crafters Guild in honor of the 1976 Bicentennial, the quilt depicts scenes in and around Montclair. It is a very successful example of a pictorial appliqué quilt crafted with plain and printed fabrics. (Montclair Crafters Guild)

Other examples of pictorial appliqué quilts are illustrated in plates 50, 67, 81, 166, 169.

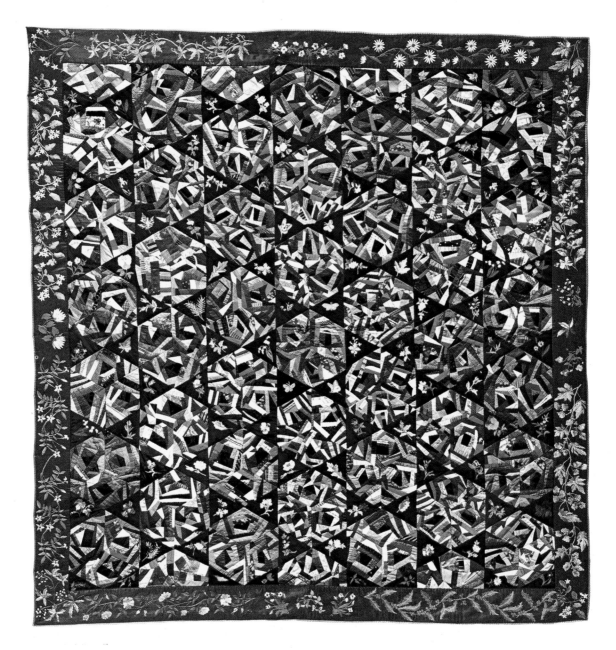

31. Pieced and embroidered quilt, Crazy, c. 1890, probably Connecticut. 86″ x 80″. Here is an astonishingly fine example of a "contained" Crazy. The slivers of fabric have been organized into diamond shapes, which are contained in hexagons, which in turn form the centers of large stars with embroidered motifs in the points. (The Connecticut Historical Society)

Other examples of Crazy quilts are illustrated in plates 26, 73, 89, 93, 140.

32. Pieced quilt, Log Cabin, Barn Raising design, c. 1890, Pennsylvania. 81″ x 81″. The white "eyes" punctuating the unusually beautiful colors in this quilt give it a unique character. (Bill Gallick and Tony Ellis)

Other examples of Log Cabin quilts are illustrated in plates 25, 52, 61, 63, 69, 90, 94, 112, 123, 125, 131, 167.

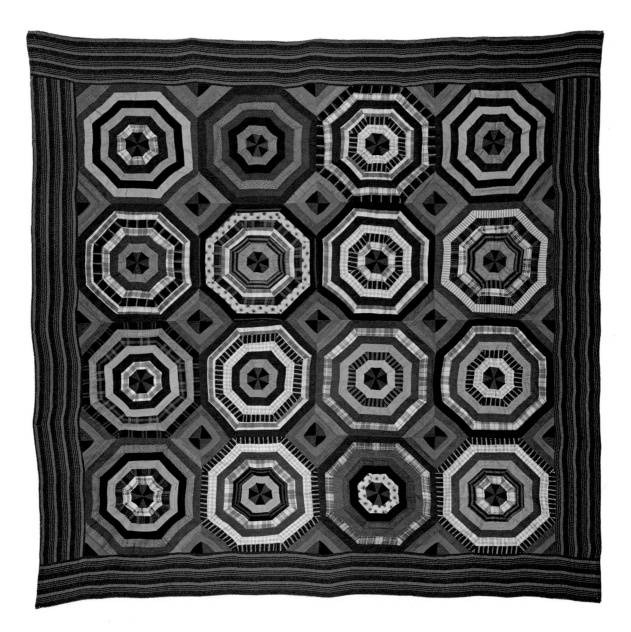

33. Pieced quilt, Cobweb, c. 1910, Pennsylvania. 83″ x 81″. Probably it is the particular shade of blue used in this quilt that makes it so strong. The blue seems to emphasize the design and fabrics of the large octagonal motifs, and the blue-and-black striped border boldly frames the whole composition. (Kelter-Malcé Antiques)

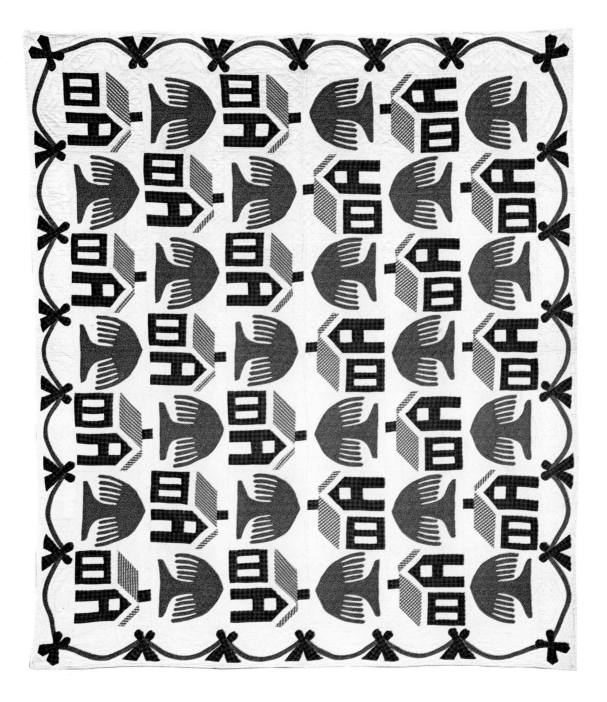

34. Pieced and appliqué quilt, Houses and Weeping Willows, c. 1880, New York State. 94″ x 82″. Symmetry, boldly patterned fabrics, and the unusual weeping-willow motif are all combined into a masterly whole. (Thos. K. Woodard: American Antiques & Quilts)

35. Appliqué quilt, unique version of Medallion, made by Ernestine Eberhardt Zaumzeil, c. 1865, Chandlerville, Illinois. 88″ x 86″. There is so much to see in this masterpiece that it deserves careful scrutiny fully to appreciate the marvelous spontaneity of its design, the color and varieties of the leaves depicted, the blossoms and berries, and the tiny animals below the central leaf design. Photograph courtesy Phyllis Haders. (George E. Schoellkopf Gallery)

Other examples of Medallion quilts are illustrated in plates 1, 2, 3, 4, 13, 36, 45, 49, 51, 54, 55, 57, 58, 70, 82, 83, 84, 99, 102, 106, 107, 108, 119, 122, 127, 128, 138, 146, 159, 164, 175, 176, 183.

36. Pieced quilt, Harlequin Medallion, calamanco, 1800–1820, New England. 87″ x 88″. The quilting in the wide border of this early nineteenth-century bedcover is truly magnificent, and it forms a splendid frame for the brightly checkered center. The quilt can be seen in the Sheldon-Hawks house at Historic Deerfield in Massachusetts. (Historic Deerfield, Inc.; Bequest of Rowena Russell Potter)

Other examples of Medallion quilts are illustrated in plates 1, 2, 3, 4, 13, 35, 45, 49, 51, 54, 55, 57, 58, 70, 82, 83, 84, 99, 102, 106, 107, 108, 119, 122, 127, 128, 138, 146, 159, 164, 175, 176, 183.

37. Pieced and appliqué quilt, Rose Spray, c. 1880, New England. 86″ x 86″. The delightfully lively floral motifs are framed with sashes composed of tiny pieced triangles in red and green and classic serpentine feather quilting in the wide border. (Phyllis Haders)

38. Pieced quilt, Bars, wool, Amish, c. 1900, Lancaster County, Pennsylvania. 84″ x 76″. Not only do we have gorgeous color in this piece, but also very fine quilting. Note especially how the feather motif in the wide borders so beautifully echoes the grapevines in the gray Bars. (Phyllis Haders)

Other examples of Amish Bars quilts are illustrated in plates 91, 132, 168.

39. Pieced quilt, Nine Patch, Mennonite, c. 1900, Holmes County, Ohio. 74″ x 65″. The artist who made this quilt certainly knew how to make the most of the play between the red and blue fabrics she used. (Barbara S. Janos)

40. Pieced quilt, Double Nine Patch, wool, Amish, 1900–1910, Lancaster County, Pennsylvania. 78″ x 78″. The color is placed with such precision in this quilt that it appears it has been created with a brush rather than with needle and thread. (Phyllis Haders)

Other examples of Nine Patch quilts are illustrated in plates 39 and 42.

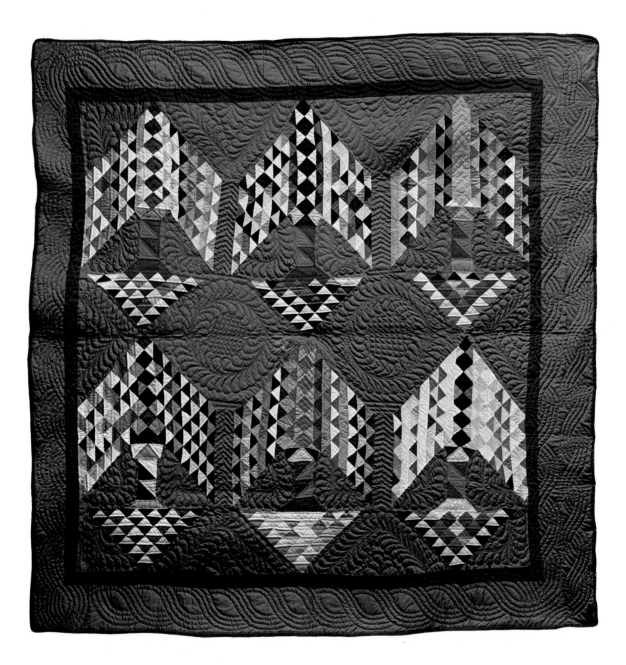

41. Pieced quilt, Tree of Life, Amish, dated 1938, Ohio. 70″ x 66½″. The Tree of Life is one of the most classic designs in American quilts. Here it is interpreted with great beauty, both in color and quilting. (Thos. K. Woodard: American Antiques & Quilts)

Other examples of Tree of Life quilts are illustrated in plates 46, 130.

Other examples of Midwestern Amish quilts are illustrated on pages 2–3 and in plates 5, 23, 62, 172.

42. Pieced quilt, Nine Patch variation, Amish, c. 1910, northern Pennsylvania. 78″ x 66″. Who can resist this piece awash with strong color and pattern? The picture-frame effect of the border is emphasized by the quilting, which is almost rococo in feeling. (America Hurrah Antiques, N.Y.C.)

Other examples of Nine Patch quilts are illustrated in plates 39, 40.

43. Pieced and appliqué quilt, Sunflowers and Double Hearts, c. 1865, New England. 91″ x 91″. This bright, happy creation cannot fail to cause a smile of pleasure. Photograph courtesy Thos. K. Woodard: American Antiques & Quilts. (Mr. and Mrs. Paul Martinson)

44. Pieced quilt, Carpenter's Wheel, c. 1890, Pennsylvania. 78″ x 72″. This quilt has it all: strong color, strong graphics, and extremely fine quilting. (America Hurrah Antiques, N.Y.C.)

45. Pieced quilt, Medallion, c. 1870, Virginia. 87″ x 78″. Note how all the motifs in this stunning variation on the Grandmother's Flower Garden design are based on the hexagon. Photograph courtesy Thos. K. Woodard: American Antiques & Quilts. (Collection of Alice Kaplan)

Other examples of Medallion quilts are illustrated in plates 1, 2, 3, 4, 13, 35, 36, 49, 51, 54, 55, 57, 58, 70, 82, 83, 84, 99, 102, 106, 107, 108, 119, 122, 127, 128, 138, 146, 159, 164, 175, 176, 183.

46. Pieced quilt, Tree of Life and Houses, c. 1900, Virginia. 78″ x 76″. This lively tapestry of color and design is one of four quilts by the same artist, all but one of which employ the same two motifs. Photograph courtesy America Hurrah Antiques, N.Y.C. (Collection of Guido Goldman)

Other examples of Tree of Life quilts are illustrated in plates 41, 130.

Other examples of House quilts are illustrated in plates 14, 34, 140.

47. Pieced quilt, Touching Stars, c. 1930, Pennsylvania. 83″ x 73″. The blues and greens in this quilt are typical of the 1930s period, as are the designs of the patterned fabrics. (Kelter-Malcé Antiques)

Other examples of Touching Star quilts are illustrated in plates 56, 76, 129, 156.

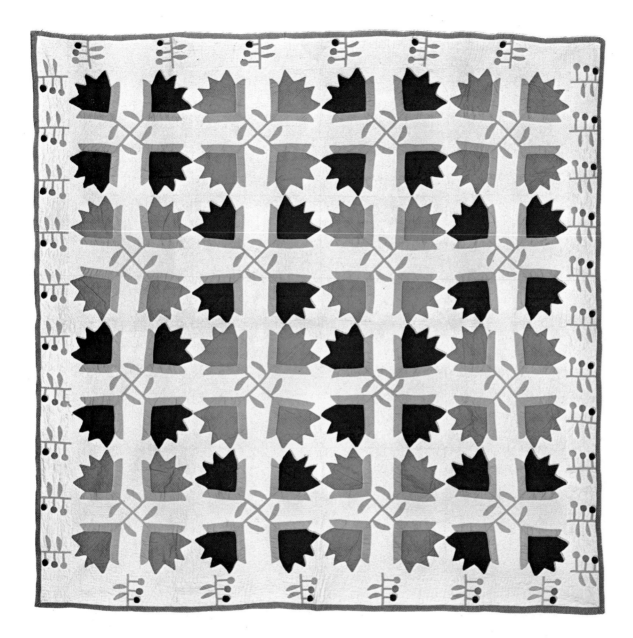

48. Appliqué quilt, Blossoms and Berries, 1880–1890, Pennsylvania. 75″ x 75″. The berries in the border are a light counterpoint to the strong forms of the blossoms. (Thos. K. Woodard: American Antiques & Quilts)

49. Pieced quilt, Medallion, c. 1870. 78″ x 74″. The artist that created this quilt obviously was an expert in modulating color and pattern to great effect. (Phyllis Haders)

Other examples of Medallion quilts are illustrated in plates 1, 2, 3, 4, 13, 35, 36, 45, 51, 54, 55, 57, 58, 70, 82, 83, 84, 99, 102, 106, 107, 108, 119, 122, 127, 128, 138, 146, 159, 164, 175, 176, 183.

50. Pieced and appliqué quilt, *Missouri Farm, Newton County,* 1975. 126″ x 102″. Designed by Edward Larson, who is represented by the Joy Horwich Gallery, Chicago, Illinois. Made by Verla Shilling, Tipton Ford, Missouri. This riot of design and color is an exciting example of a contemporary artist working in the quilt medium. Photograph courtesy the artist. (Private collection)

Other examples of pictorial appliqué quilts are illustrated in plates 30, 64, 67, 81, 166, 169.

51. Pieced quilt top, Medallion with Odd Fellows' Cross in center, c. 1875, Maryland. 86″ x 84″. The creator of this extraordinary quilt top powerfully concentrates one's attention on the center not only through the series of borders diminishing in size, but also by the four strong diagonals. (Thos. K. Woodard: American Antiques & Quilts)

Other examples of Medallion quilts are illustrated in plates 1, 2, 3, 4, 13, 35, 36, 45, 49, 54, 55, 57, 58, 70, 82, 83, 84, 99, 102, 106, 107, 108, 119, 122, 127, 128, 138, 146, 159, 164, 175, 176, 183.

52. Pieced quilt, Log Cabin, Barn Raising design, c. 1910, Pennsylvania. 88″ x 70″. Here is a particularly strong, gutsy interpretation of the popular Barn Raising design. (Kelter-Malcé Antiques)

Other examples of Log Cabin quilts are illustrated in plates 25, 32, 61, 63, 69, 90, 94, 112, 123, 125, 131, 167.

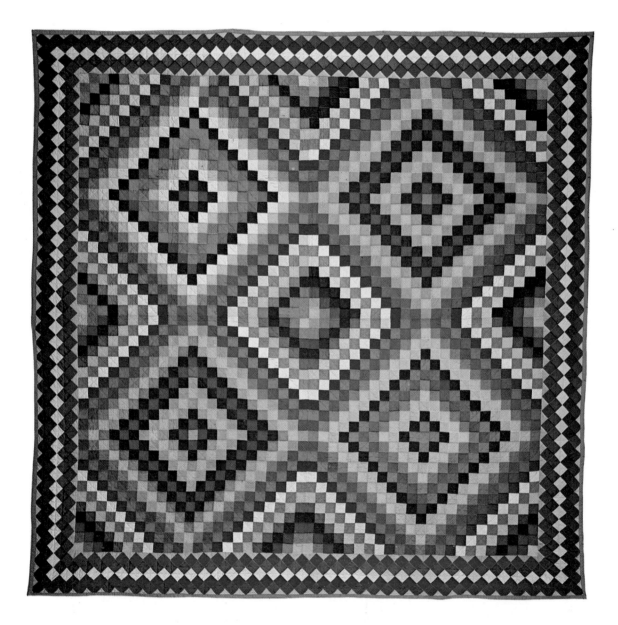

53. Pieced quilt, Philadelphia Pavement variation, c. 1950, Pennsylvania. 82″ x 82″. Clearly, the quilter who made this piece was determined to stun us with dazzling color. (America Hurrah Antiques, N.Y.C.)

54. Crewel-embroidered wool coverlet, Medallion, 1815–1830, New England. 100″ x 84″. Here is a marvelous specimen of a rare species. Bold design, great color, and exceptional needlework all combine to make this a magnificent bedcover. Compare this example to the very similar piece illustrated in plate 119. Photograph courtesy Thos. K. Woodard: American Antiques & Quilts. (Private collection)

Other examples of Medallion quilts are illustrated in plates 1, 2, 3, 4, 13, 35, 36, 45, 49, 51, 55, 57, 58, 70, 82, 83, 84, 99, 102, 106, 107, 108, 119, 122, 127, 128, 138, 146, 159, 164, 175, 176, 183.

55. Pieced quilt, Mosaic Medallion, c. 1840. 126″ x 120″. Obviously, almost any quilt requires a large amount of careful planning to ensure a successful result; however, the mind boggles at the work that must have gone into the creation of this enormous, complex flowing design made of early printed cottons. Photograph courtesy George E. Schoellkopf Gallery. (Private collection)

Other examples of Medallion quilts are illustrated in plates, 1, 2, 3, 4, 13, 35, 36, 45, 49, 51, 54, 57, 58, 70, 82, 83, 84, 99, 102, 106, 107, 108, 119, 122, 127, 128, 138, 146, 159, 164, 175, 176, 183.

56. Pieced quilt, Touching Stars, c. 1845, Pennsylvania. 102″ x 102″. The sumptuous effect of this quilt is emphasized by the gorgeous color in the wide chintz border and by the handsome quilting throughout. (Kelter-Malcé Antiques)

Other examples of Touching Stars quilts are illustrated in plates 47, 76, 129, 156.

57. Crewel-embroidered wool blanket, Medallion, 1790–1810, New England. 90¾″ x 90″. Here is a perfect example of country crewel: airy, informal, colorful, imaginative. (The Henry Francis du Pont Winterthur Museum)

Other examples of Medallion quilts are illustrated in plates 1, 2, 3, 4, 13, 35, 36, 45, 49, 51, 54, 55, 58, 70, 82, 83, 84, 99, 102, 106, 107, 108, 119, 122, 127, 128, 138, 146, 159, 164, 175, 176, 183.

58. White stuffed-work coverlet, Medallion, 1810–1820, Pennsylvania. 97½″ x 90″. Exquisite needlework and a classic design full of fascinating details combine to create a first-rate example of "white work." The central design of the piece is the very popular motif of a vase or basket of flowers, also seen, for instance, in plates 54, 57, 70, and 119. Photograph courtesy America Hurrah Antiques, N.Y.C. (Private collection)

Other examples of quilts with stuffed work are illustrated in plates 3, 10, 12, 74, 99, 100, 146, 180.

Other examples of Medallion quilts are illustrated in plates 1, 2, 3, 4, 13, 35, 36, 45, 49, 51, 54, 55, 57, 70, 82, 83, 84, 99, 102, 106, 107, 108, 119, 122, 127, 128, 138, 146, 159, 164, 175, 176, 183.

59. Pieced and appliqué quilt, unique design, c. 1860, Pennsylvania. 97″ x 107″. As in the quilt illustrated in plate 35, the creator of this piece was fascinated by leaves. But in contrast to the flowing spontaneity of the Zaumzeil quilt, this interpretation is precise and orderly, qualities that are underlined by the pieced blocks and their subtle colors. (Thos. K. Woodard: American Antiques & Quilts)

60. Pieced and appliqué quilt, Pot of Flowers, c. 1860, Ohio. 78″ x 78″. "Fat and sassy" is probably the best description for the central motif in this stunning quilt. (America Hurrah Antiques, N.Y.C.)

Other examples of Pot of Flowers quilts are illustrated in plates 15, 20, 21, 149, 157, 173, 181.

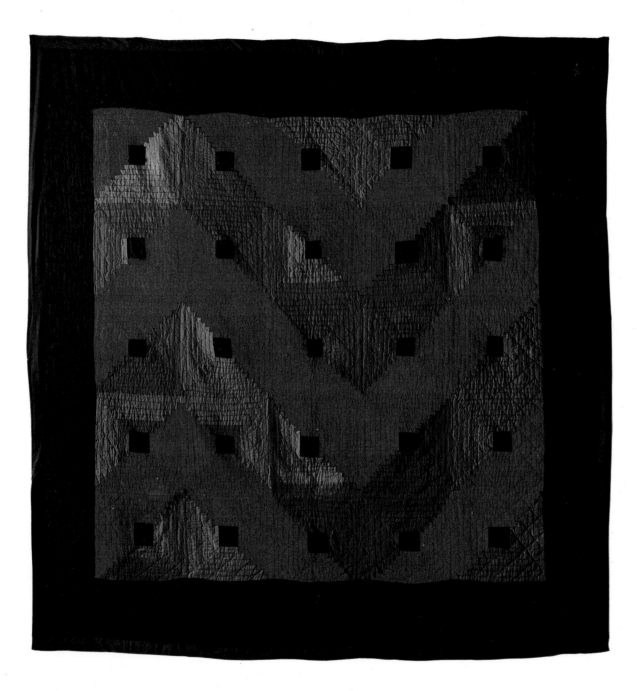

61. Pieced quilt, Log Cabin, Streak o' Lightning design, c. 1910, Pennsylvania. 84″ x 78″. Here the popular red and green color scheme is made unforgettable by the stunning bold scale of the design. (Kelter-Malcé Antiques)

Other examples of Log Cabin quilts are illustrated in plates 25, 32, 52, 63, 69, 90, 94, 112, 123, 125, 131, 167.

62. Pieced quilt, Amish Railroad Crossing, c. 1920, Indiana. 80″ x 78″. The dark background of the quilt emphasizes the brilliant, jewellike effect of the slivers of color. Photograph courtesy Kelter-Malcé Antiques. (Private collection)

Other examples of Midwestern Amish quilts are illustrated on pages 2–3 and in plates 5, 23, 172.

63. Pieced and appliqué quilt, silk and embroidery, Log Cabin variation, c. 1870, found in New Jersey. 76″ x 62″. This is an imaginative and important example of black folk art. Note the log cabin in the center with the rosebush growing at the side, the more than 100 houses, and the many blocks with black figures shown in various daily pursuits. The creator of this quilt was quite possibly a professional dressmaker who had access to scraps of silk. Photograph courtesy Thos. K. Woodard: American Antiques & Quilts. (Private collection)

Other examples of Log Cabin quilts are illustrated in plates 25, 32, 52, 61, 69, 90, 94, 112, 123, 125, 131, 167.

64. Pieced and appliqué quilt, unique design, 1916, Middlefield, Massachusetts. 90″ x 74″. Based on comic-strip characters of the period, this quilt was made as a family project by the four children of Augustine and Jane Savery. (Thos. K. Woodard: American Antiques & Quilts)

Other examples of pictorial appliqué quilts are illustrated in plates 30, 50, 67, 81, 166, 169.

65. Pieced and appliqué crib quilt with a Sawtooth Star centering each large block, c. 1865. 44¾" x 39½". The red calicoes in this piece show a subtle gradation of color and are handsomely set off by the yellow and green prints. (America Hurrah Antiques, N.Y.C.)

Other examples of crib quilts are illustrated in plates 16, 28, 75, 111, 150, 165.

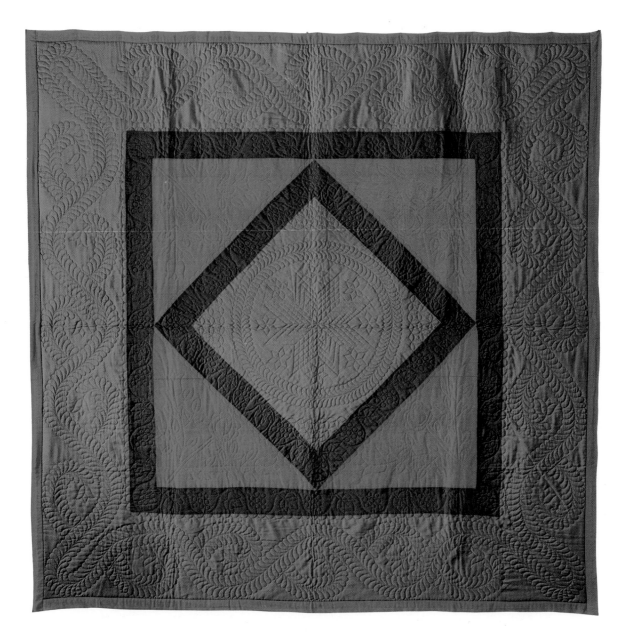

66. Pieced quilt, Center Diamond, wool, Amish, c. 1910, Lancaster County, Pennsylvania. 82″ x 82″. The red-orange, brown, and slate-blue palette is most unusual and very beautiful. The serpentine-feather quilting in the wide border includes tulips. Photograph courtesy Thos. K. Woodard: American Antiques & Quilts. (Private collection)

Other examples of Amish Center Diamond quilts are illustrated in plates 6, 8, 97, 124, 126, 142, 154.

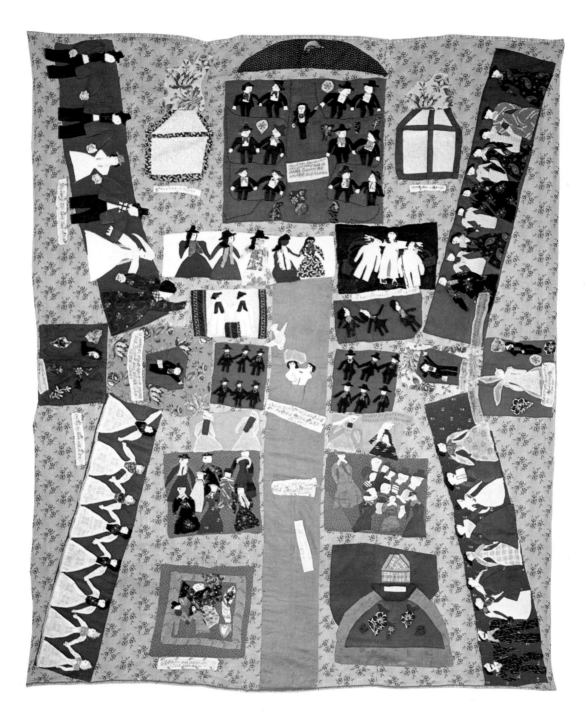

67. Appliqué quilt, inscribed "Sacret Bibel Quilt," made by Susan Arrowood, c. 1895, West Chester, Pennsylvania. 90″ x 72″. Inspired by deep religious feelings, this extraordinary piece depicts (according to the maker's labels on the quilt with her very own spelling) such events as (center) "John Baptizing Jesus in the river off Jorden," (top center) "Jesus on the mountain sending his desiples threw the world to preach," and (far left) "Jesus in the garden praying." Photograph courtesy Thos. K. Woodard: American Antiques & Quilts. (Private collection)

Other examples of pictorial appliqué quilts are illustrated in plates 30, 50, 64, 81, 166, 169.

68. Appliqué quilt, Water Lily, c. 1930, West Virginia. 76″ x 76″. This is a particularly pleasing example of a quilt made from a commercial pattern. The quilting is beautifully done. Photograph courtesy Frederick Di Maio: Inglenook Antiques. (Private collection)

69. Pieced quilt, Log Cabin, Straight Furrow design, c. 1925, Pennsylvania. 70″ x 70″. The black-and-white striped material that has been pieced so imaginatively and the red "eyes" give a strong, modern feeling to this quilt. (America Hurrah Antiques, N.Y.C.)

Other examples of Log Cabin quilts are illustrated in plates 25, 32, 52, 61, 63, 90, 94, 122, 123, 125, 131, 167.

70. Appliqué spread, Medallion, 1840–1850, New York State. 84″ x 100″. This garland of floral beauty is a particularly soft and lovely creation. (Thos. K. Woodard: American Antiques & Quilts)

Other examples of Medallion quilts are illustrated in plates 1, 2, 3, 4, 13, 35, 36, 45, 49, 51, 54, 55, 57, 58, 82, 83, 84, 99, 102, 106, 107, 108, 119, 122, 127, 128, 138, 146, 159, 164, 175, 176, 183.

71. Pieced and appliqué quilt, unique design, c. 1850, New York State. 62″ x 74″. Whoever made this quilt obviously had a special love for horses. Note the outlines of a turkey in the lower right corner. The piece is a particularly interesting example of folk art in quilts. Photograph courtesy America Hurrah Antiques, N.Y.C. (Private collection)

72. Pieced quilt, Brick Wall in zigzag arrangement, c. 1910, Midwest. 73″ x 66″. There is such brilliant energy in this quilt, it almost appears to be electrically charged. (Thos. K. Woodard: American Antiques & Quilts)

73. Pieced quilt, Crazy, silk, c. 1880, Michigan. 60″ x 50″. A superior example of a "contained" Crazy, this piece has a fiendishly clever design that combines Tumbling Blocks with Hexagon Stars. (Kelter-Malcé Antiques)

Other examples of Crazy quilts are illustrated in plates 26, 31, 89, 93, 140.

Other examples of Tumbling Blocks quilts are illustrated in plates 103, 111.

74. Appliqué quilt with stuffed work, Album, dated 1860. 82″ x 73″. This gorgeous piece is remarkable for the exquisite quality of the stuffed work, for the beauty of the many-layered appliqués, and for the delightful variety in the design of the border. As if that were not enough, the following inscription forms an inner border of stuffed work: "1860. Done by Mrs. C. Bartlett in the 63 year of her age. Name true American." The little red dots seen in this inner border separate many of the words in the inscription. Photograph courtesy America Hurrah Antiques, N.Y.C. (Private collection)

Other examples of Album quilts are illustrated in plates 4, 7, 80, 87, 115, 147, 174.

Other examples of stuffed work are illustrated in plates, 3, 10, 12, 58, 99, 100, 146, 180.

75. Pieced child's quilt, Star, c. 1830, Connecticut. 60″ x 58″. This gem incorporates a sumptuous group of early printed cottons and chintzes. Photograph courtesy Kelter-Malcé Antiques. (Private collection)

Other examples of crib quilts are illustrated in plates 16, 28, 65, 111, 150, 165.

Other examples of Star quilts are illustrated in plates 20, 22, 78, 79, 85, 116, 118, 129, 134, 143, 144, 152, 165, 170, 171, 178, 179, 185.

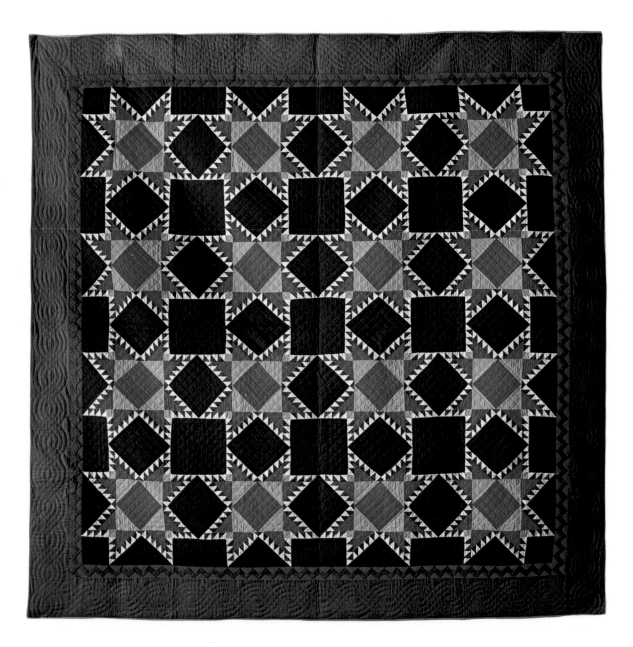

76. Pieced quilt, Touching Stars, Mennonite, c. 1890, Berks County, Pennsylvania. 80″ x 80″. Brilliantly conceived, the white "feathers" on the stars add extra dazzle to an already stunning quilt. Photograph courtesy America Hurrah Antiques, N.Y.C. (Private collection)

Other examples of Touching Stars quilts are illustrated in plates 47, 56, 129, 156.

77. Pieced quilt, Zigzag, Mennonite, c. 1890, Pennsylvania. 102″ x 84″. Surely this eyeful must be the supreme example of a Zigzag quilt! (Thos. K. Woodard: American Antiques & Quilts)

78. Pieced quilt, Blazing Star, chintz, 1830–1840. 94″ x 94″. The quilt should be closely examined to appreciate the skill with which the pieces have been cut to heighten the blazing effect. (America Hurrah Antiques, N.Y.C.)

Other examples of Star quilts are illustrated in plates 20, 22, 75, 79, 85, 106, 116, 118, 129, 134, 143, 144, 152, 165, 170, 171, 178, 179, 185.

79. Pieced quilt, Star, wool, Amish, c. 1890, Ohio. 76″ x 83″. Unusual color and bold design make this the pride of any quilt collection—or painting collection, for that matter. (Phyllis Haders)

Other examples of Star quilts are illustrated in plates 20, 22, 75, 78, 85, 106, 116, 118, 129, 134, 143, 144, 152, 165, 170, 171, 178, 179, 185.

80. Appliqué quilt, Album, 1845–1855. 104″ x 88″. The double-circle format, the color and execution of the motifs, and the splendid border make this an exceptional quilt. (America Hurrah Antiques, N.Y.C.)

Other examples of Album quilts are illustrated in plates 4,7, 74,87, 115, 147, 174.

81. Appliqué quilt, designed by Curt Boehringer, Chesterland, Ohio, and made by Fran Soika, 1981, Novelty, Ohio. 94″ x 68″. Made for The Gates Mills Community Club in Ohio, this contemporary pictorial appliqué quilt depicts the town and countryside of Gates Mills, Ohio. (The Gates Mills Community Club)

Other pictorial appliqué quilts are illustrated in plates 30, 50, 64, 67, 166, 169.

82. Pieced quilt, Harlequin Medallion, calamanco, 1810–1820, New England. 86¾″ x 96″. It seems astonishing that such an early quilt could be so modern in its aesthetic sensibility. Calamanco is a glossy woolen fabric. Photograph courtesy George E. Schoellkopf Gallery. (Private collection)

Other examples of Medallion quilts are illustrated in plates 1, 2, 3, 4, 13, 35, 36, 45, 49, 51, 54, 55, 57, 58, 70, 83, 84, 99, 102, 106, 107, 108, 119, 122, 127, 128, 138, 146, 159, 164, 175, 176, 183.

83. Pieced and appliqué Royal Hawaiian quilt in Medallion style, called *Ku'u Hae Aloha* (*My Beloved Flag*), 1900–1910, Hawaiian Islands. 74″ x 74″. This type of Hawaiian quilt was made as an act of patriotism after the abdication of the Hawaiian queen and the subsequent lowering of the Hawaiian flag. It is a great rarity and very handsome. Photograph courtesy Thos. K. Woodard: American Antiques & Quilts. (Kiracofe and Kile)

Other examples of Medallion quilts are illustrated in plates 1, 2, 3, 4, 13, 35, 36, 45, 49, 51, 54, 55, 57, 58, 70, 82, 84, 99, 102, 106, 107, 108, 119, 122, 127, 128, 138, 146, 159, 164, 175, 176, 183.

84. Pieced and appliqué quilt, Medallion, c. 1900, from the Marie Landis family, Lancaster County, Pennsylvania. 80″ x 78″. This great splash of free-form design and color features checkerboard ducks in the border and what might be construed as two very abstract peacocks below the central tulip. (Bettie Mintz: All of Us Americans Folk Art)

Other examples of Medallion quilts are illustrated in plates 1, 2, 3, 4, 13, 35, 36, 45, 49, 51, 54, 55, 57, 58, 70, 82, 83, 99, 102, 106, 107, 108, 119, 122, 127, 128, 138, 146, 159, 164, 175, 176, 183.

85. Pieced quilt, Star of Bethlehem, 1865–1875, New England. 85½″ x 85½″. The particular fascination of this quilt is the way that the areas between the points of the star have been filled with small pieced diamonds that give the effect of being "leftovers" after the central star was created. Needless to say, the color scheme is especially brilliant. (America Hurrah Antiques, N.Y.C.)

Other examples of Star quilts are illustrated in plates 20, 22, 75, 78, 79, 106, 116, 118, 129, 134, 143, 144, 152, 165, 170, 171, 178, 179, 185.

86. Pieced quilt, c. 1850, Connecticut. 88¼" x 66½". Some of the most satisfying quilts are those that use a wide variety of blue fabrics with a white background. The small triangles act effectively as grace notes to the larger geometrics in this piece. Photograph courtesy George E. Schoellkopf Gallery. (Private collection)

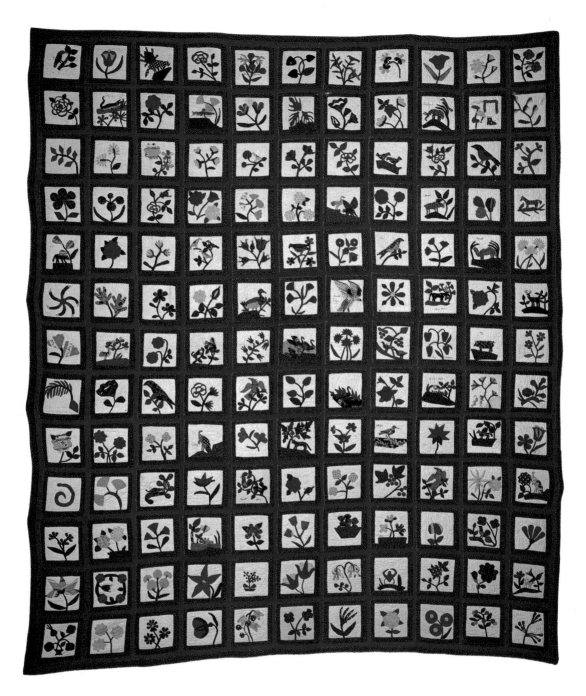

87. Pieced and appliqué quilt, Album, 1850–1860, New York State. Among the fascinating calico creatures that inhabit this great quilt are many birds, a grasshopper, an elephant, a camel, and a stag. Photograph courtesy Thos. K. Woodard: American Antiques & Quilts. (Private collection)

Other examples of Album quilts are illustrated in plates 4, 7, 74, 80, 115, 147, 174.

88. Pieced and appliqué quilt, made by Harriet J. Dishong with the assistance of Mrs. Mary E. Dishong, near McConnellsburg, Fulton County, Pennsylvania. This masterpiece of American folk art was started in 1875 and completed March 20, 1890, and the latter date is embroidered on the Bible appliquéd on the large brown heart in the center of the right border. 94¼" x 88½". This extraordinary creation contains 22,640 pieces of fabric in the central panel, including 21,672 triangles measuring ½" x ¾". On the wide borders are appliquéd all manner of objects: birds, butterflies, insects, fruit, vegetables, a watch, a pocketknife, scissors, etc. Photograph courtesy Morgan Lee Anderson. (America Hurrah Antiques, N.Y.C.)

89. Pieced and appliqué quilt, Crazy, c. 1900, Pennsylvania. 76″ x 64″. This quilt was first published in the 1976 calendar, and it still is one of the most interesting and colorful Crazy quilts I have seen. The appliqué motifs are in the Orange Peel design. (Kelter-Malcé Antiques)

Other examples of Crazy quilts are illustrated in plates 26, 31, 73, 93, 140.

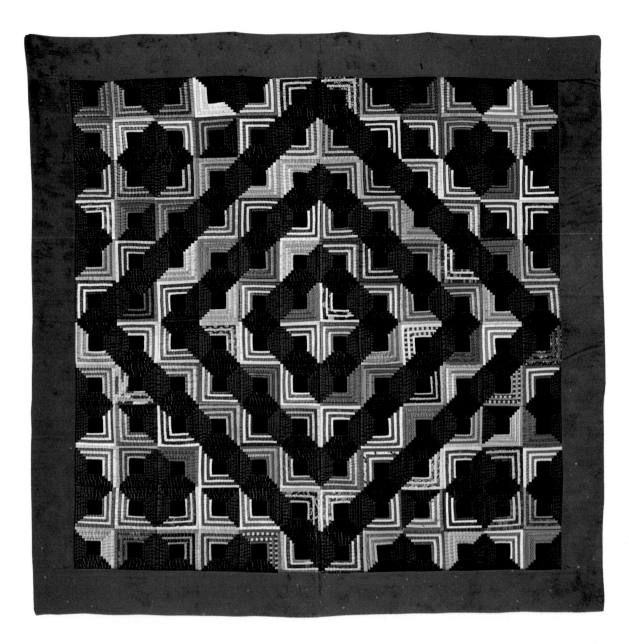

90. Pieced quilt, Log Cabin, Barn Raising design, silk and velvet, c. 1890. 63″ x 63″.
In perfect condition and with the silks still as bright as jewels, this is a breathtaking
example of the elegant Victorian parlor throws created in the Log Cabin style.
(Frederick Di Maio: Inglenook Antiques)

Other examples of Log Cabin quilts are illustrated in plates 25, 32, 52, 61, 63, 69, 94,
112, 123, 125, 131, 167.

91. Pieced quilt, Bars, wool, Amish, c. 1890, Lancaster County, Pennsylvania. 82″ x 74″. Amish quilts of this quality are greatly treasured because of their beauty as fabric paintings. (Thos. K. Woodard: American Antiques & Quilts)

Other examples of Amish Bars quilts are illustrated in plates 38, 132, 168.

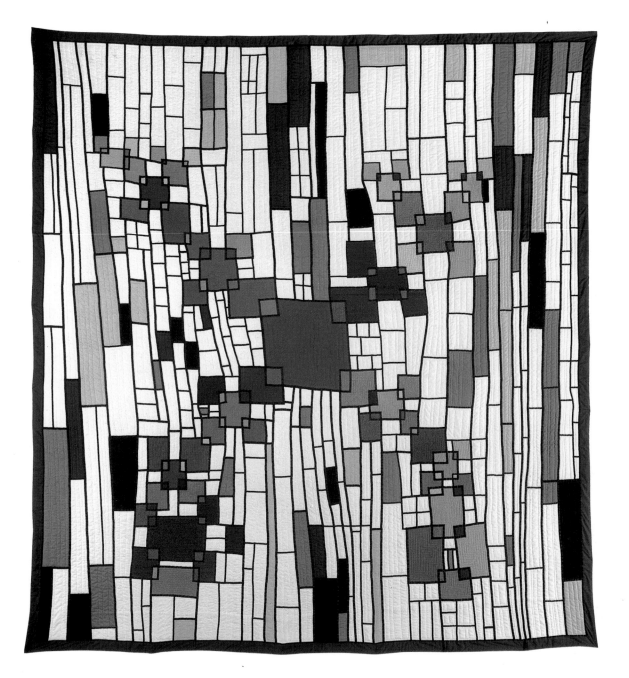

92. Pieced and appliqué quilt, *Public Square*, designed and made by Fran Soika, 1980, Novelty, Ohio. 114″ x 106″. With a design adapted from a watercolor made by her daughter, this wonderful contemporary piece displays a great sensitivity to color values as well as to abstract form. The quilt is hand-pieced and hand-quilted, and the divisions in the quilt are made with appliquéd black satin ribbon. (Collection of the artist)

93. Pieced quilt, Crazy, wool and flannel, 1900–1910, Lancaster, Pennsylvania. 78″ x 73″. Made by a country woman, this quilt shows an intuitive sense of the power of abstract design and color that is very modern. Photograph courtesy America Hurrah Antiques, N.Y.C. (Private collection)

Other examples of Crazy quilts are illustrated in plates 26, 31, 73, 89, 140.

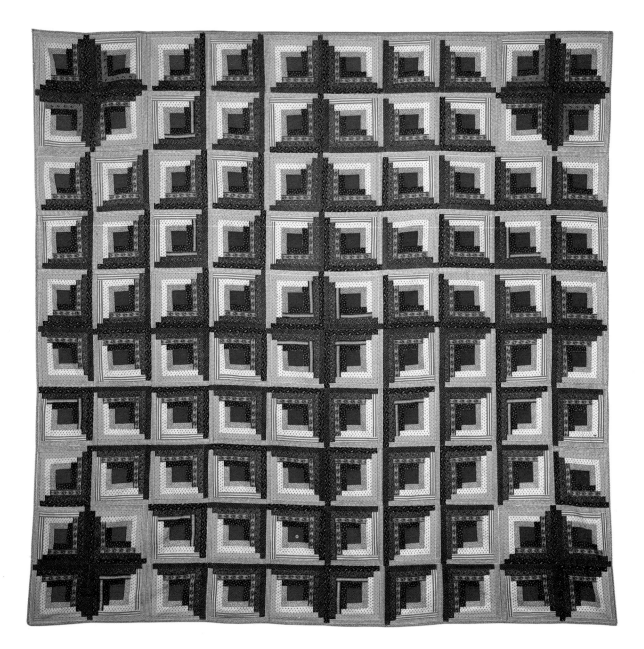

94. Pieced quilt, Log Cabin in Barn Raising variation, c. 1880, Pennsylvania. 84″ x 84″. The color, control, and energy of this piece make it one of the very great Log Cabin quilts. (America Hurrah Antiques, N.Y.C.)

Other examples of Log Cabin quilts are illustrated in plates 25, 32, 52, 61, 63, 69, 90, 112, 123, 125, 131, 167.

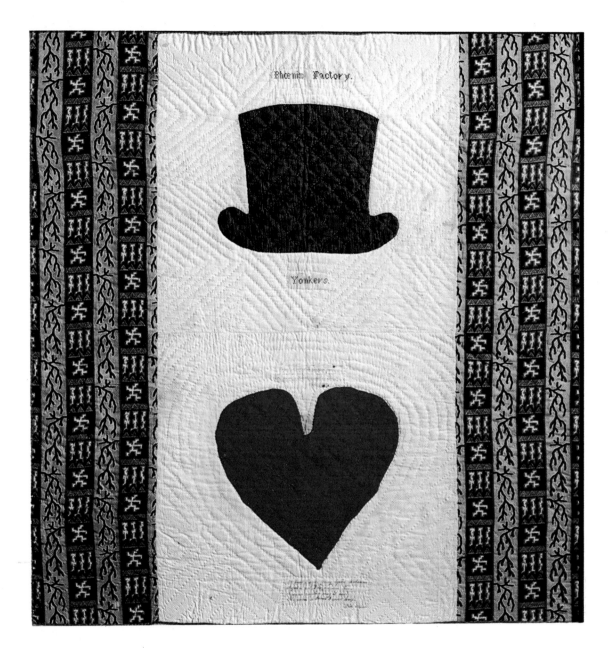

95. Appliqué quilted valentine with chintz borders, c. 1850, Yonkers, New York. 34½″ x 32½″. Above the hat is written "Phoenix Factory"; under it the word "Yonkers." Above and below the heart is written (with minor variations in the wording) "A Heart I send you Squire Baldwine/ Reject it not I do implore thee/ A warm reception may it meet/ My name a secret I must keep" [Signed] "Old Maid." This is one of the most touching documents in American quilts, and it has inspired a contemporary quilt created as a wedding gift, which is illustrated in plate 122. Photograph courtesy Gary C. Cole. (David Davies)

96. Pieced quilt, designed and pieced by Nancy Crow and hand-quilted by Mrs. Levi Mast under the artist's supervision. © 1980, Baltimore, Ohio. 38″ x 38″. Titled *Bittersweet IV:* "Intensity Deepening," this vibrant work is one of a series of eleven quilts that form the chronology of a relationship. Photograph courtesy the artist. (Collection of the artist)

97. Pieced quilt, Center Diamond, wool, Amish, 1910, Lancaster County, Pennsylvania. 80″ x 78″. This book contains eight Amish Center Diamond quilts, and each is a testament to the intuitive handling of color by Amish quilters. (America Hurrah Antiques, N.Y.C.)

Other examples of Amish Center Diamond quilts are illustrated in plates 6, 8, 66, 124, 126, 142, 154.

98. Pieced quilt, *Norfolk Hue*, designed and made by Jacqueline Schuman, 1978, New York City. 102″ x 77½″. This artist's quilt, made in the Thousand Pyramids design, is a scintillating expression of color and texture. (Collection of the artist)

99. Appliqué quilt, Broderie Perse/Medallion with stuffed work, c. 1825. 118¾" x 123". Flowers, butterflies, birds, and even a bird's nest inhabit the exquisite chintz cutouts that decorate this elegant confection. (The Henry Francis du Pont Winterthur Museum)

Other examples of Broderie Perse quilts are illustrated in plates 3, 128, 130, 145.

Other examples of quilts with stuffed work are illustrated in plates 3, 10, 12, 58, 74, 100, 146, 180.

Other examples of Medallion quilts are illustrated in plates 1, 2, 3, 4, 13, 35, 36, 45, 49, 51, 54, 55, 57, 58, 70, 82, 83, 84, 102, 106, 107, 108, 119, 122, 127, 128, 138, 146, 159, 164, 175, 176, 183.

100. Pieced quilt, Feathered Star, c. 1850, made by a member of the Hunt family, Waynesville, Warren County, Ohio. 92″ x 95″. The glory of this piece is the marvelous stuffed work, particularly the broad border with the unusual motif of classic urns framed by flowers and leaves. All aspects of this quilt combine beautifully to create its unmistakable character of being a treasured heirloom. (Warren County Historical Society)

Other examples of Feathered Star quilts are illustrated in plates 129, 178.

Other examples of quilts with stuffed work are illustrated in plates 3, 10, 12, 58, 74, 99, 146, 180.

101. Pieced quilt, Old Maid's Ramble, c. 1885, Pennsylvania. 76" x 76". The fascination of this exercise in geometrics is the intermingling of stars-within-stars and squares-within-squares, achieved with the simplest of forms—squares and triangles. (America Hurrah Antiques, N.Y.C.)

102. Pieced quilt top, Medallion, 1870–1880, Massachusetts. 86″ x 84½″. Here is another extraordinary combination of squares and triangles in both plain and printed fabrics. The result is not only handsome in its own terms but is also very contemporary in its aesthetic appeal. Photograph courtesy Kelter-Malcé Antiques. (Museum of American Folk Art)

Other examples of Medallion quilts are illustrated in plates 1, 2, 3, 4, 13, 35, 36, 45, 49, 51, 54, 55, 57, 58, 70, 82, 83, 84, 99, 106, 107, 108, 119, 122, 127, 128, 138, 146, 159, 164, 175, 176, 183.

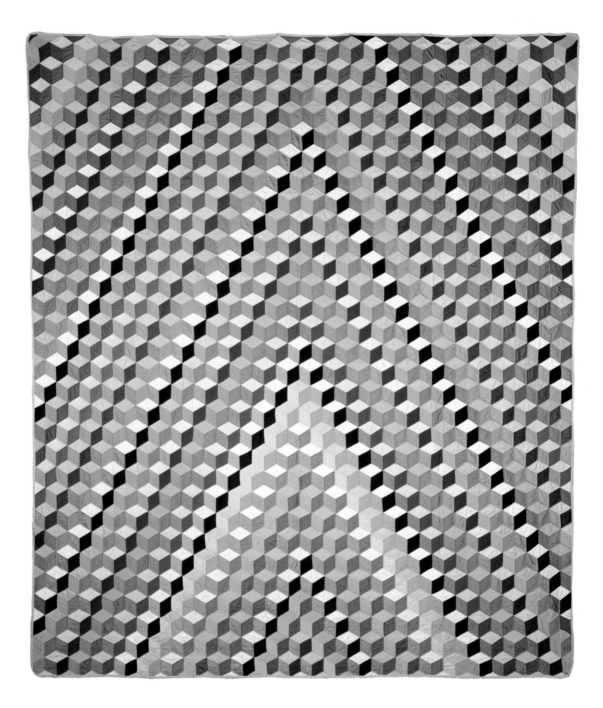

103. Pieced quilt, Tumbling Blocks, Amish, 1930–1940, Ohio. 108″ x 94″. Surely this is the zenith of a Tumbling Blocks quilt, so brilliant in its crescendo of color and form. (America Hurrah Antiques, N.Y.C.)

Other examples of Tumbling Blocks quilts are illustrated in plates 73, 111.

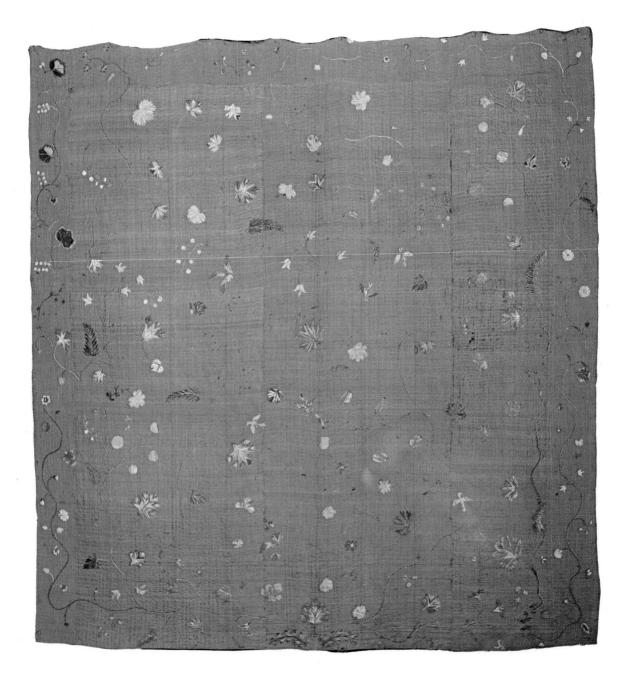

104. Coverlet of linsey-woolsey (a heavy fabric woven of linen and wool) with crewel-embroidered flowers and birds, c. 1800, New England. 88″ x 85″. The special appeal of American crewel embroidery is its airy informality. What makes this piece so entrancing is the way the flowers have been scattered over its surface with complete abandon, much as one finds wildflowers growing in a meadow. Photograph courtesy James Mincemoyer. (Private collection)

105. Pieced quilt, *Four Papaver Against an Azure Sky*, designed and pieced by Nancy Crow, 1977, Baltimore, Ohio, and hand-quilted by Velma Brill under the artist's supervision. Nancy Crow has achieved wide recognition as one of America's most stimulating and accomplished artists using the quilt medium. This interpretation of Oriental poppies (botanical name: *Papaver*) against a sky of bright blue was the artist's first quilt using the strip-piecing method. Photograph courtesy The Canton Art Institute. (The Massillon Museum)

106. Pieced quilt of glazed linsey-woolsey, Star/Medallion, c. 1800, New York State. 101″ x 99″. First published in the 1975 *Quilt Calendar*, this remains one of the finest pieced linseys to come to light. It is a superior example because of the boldness of its design, color, and quilting. Photograph courtesy Cora Ginsburg, Benjamin Ginsburg—Antiquary. (Private collection)

Other examples of Star quilts are illustrated in plates 20, 22, 78, 79, 85, 116, 118, 129, 134, 143, 144, 152, 165, 170, 171, 178, 179, 185.

Other examples of Medallion quilts are illustrated in plates 1, 2, 3, 4, 13, 35, 36, 45, 49, 51, 54, 55, 57, 58, 70, 82, 83, 84, 99, 102, 107, 108, 119, 122, 127, 128, 138, 146, 159, 164, 175, 176, 183.

107. Appliqué quilt, Medallion, 1865–1875, Pennsylvania. 96″ x 87″. Striking Pennsylvania color and unusual contour quilting in the large central panel give a special "brio" to this boldly designed floral fantasy. (America Hurrah Antiques, N.Y.C.)

Other examples of Medallion quilts are illustrated in plates 1, 2, 3, 4, 13, 35, 36, 45, 49, 51, 54, 55, 57, 58, 70, 82, 83, 84, 99, 102, 106, 108, 119, 122, 127, 128, 138, 146, 159, 164, 175, 176, 183.

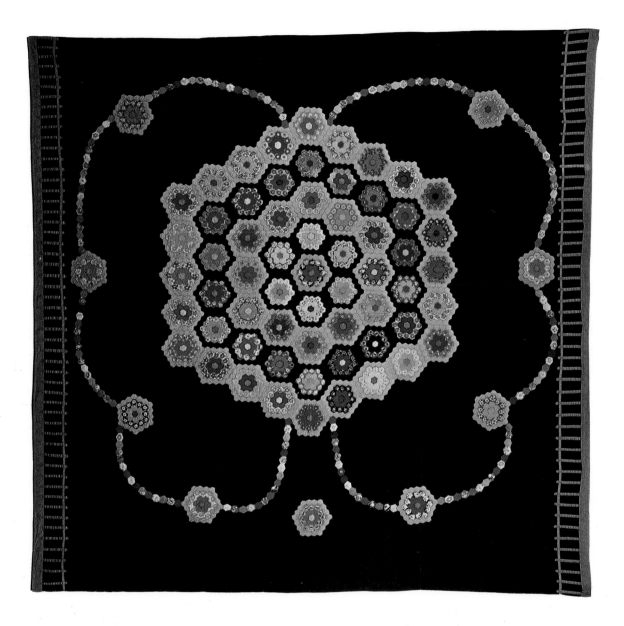

108. Pieced quilt, Medallion/Grandmother's Flower Garden, c. 1930. 82″ x 84″. Talk about imagination and creativity! Here is a delightfully formal garden linked by surrounding paths to satellite gardens, with what is perhaps intended as a fountain set at lower center in front of the entrance to the garden. Justifiably, this gem is protected by a picket-fence border. Photograph courtesy Wild Goose Chase Quilt Gallery. (Collection of Gary Brockman)

Other examples of Medallion quilts are illustrated in plates 1, 2, 3, 4, 13, 35, 36, 45, 49, 51, 54, 55, 57, 58, 70, 82, 83, 84, 99, 102, 106, 107, 119, 122, 127, 128, 138, 146, 159, 164, 175, 176, 183.

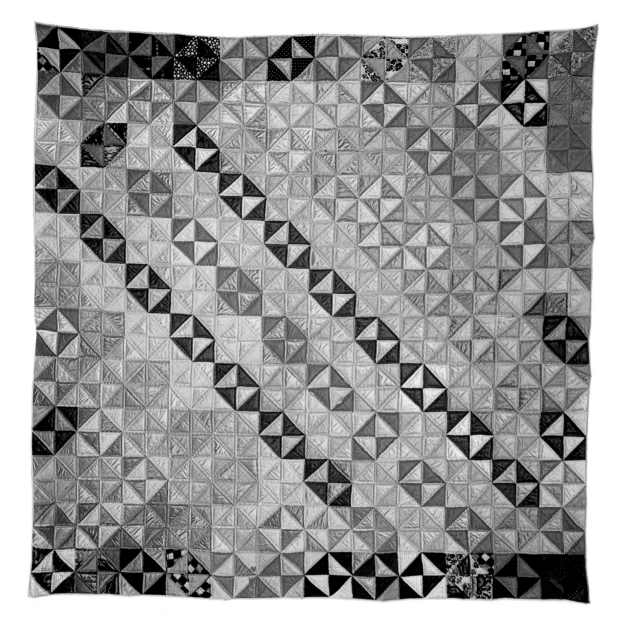

109. Pieced quilt, Broken Dishes, silk, c. 1920. 77″ x 77″. The simplest of pieced designs here becomes memorable because of the expert placement of luscious color. (Phyllis Haders)

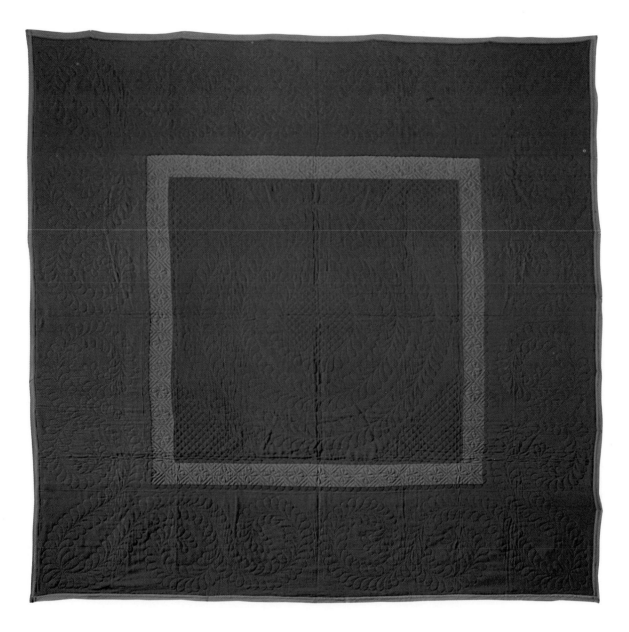

110. Pieced quilt, Center Square, wool, Amish, c. 1895, Lancaster County, Pennsylvania. 82″ x 82″. This masterpiece of color and texture is a very great example of an Amish quilted "painting." Photograph courtesy America Hurrah Antiques, N.Y.C. (Private collection)

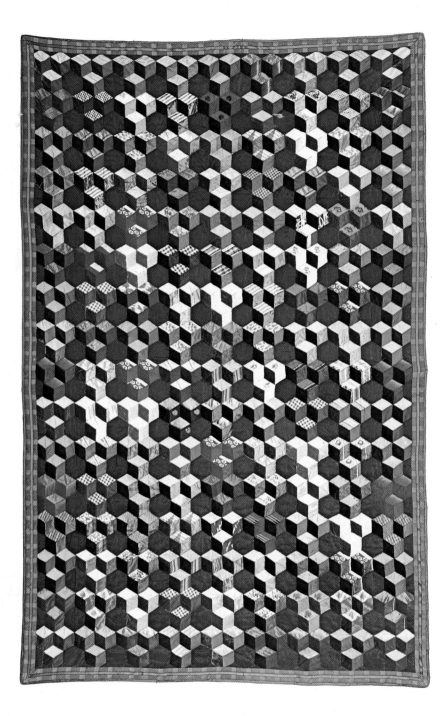

111. Pieced crib quilt, Tumbling Blocks, c. 1890. 60¾″ x 38½″. In this superb quilt the bright three-block units have been used to create columns with a strong architectural feeling. The rows of dark hexagons separating the columns emphasize the beauty of the color that flickers throughout the quilt. Photograph courtesy George E. Schoellkopf Gallery. (Malcolm Kirk)

Other examples of Tumbling Blocks quilts are illustrated in plates 73, 103.

Other examples of crib quilts are illustrated in plates 16, 28, 65, 75, 150, 165.

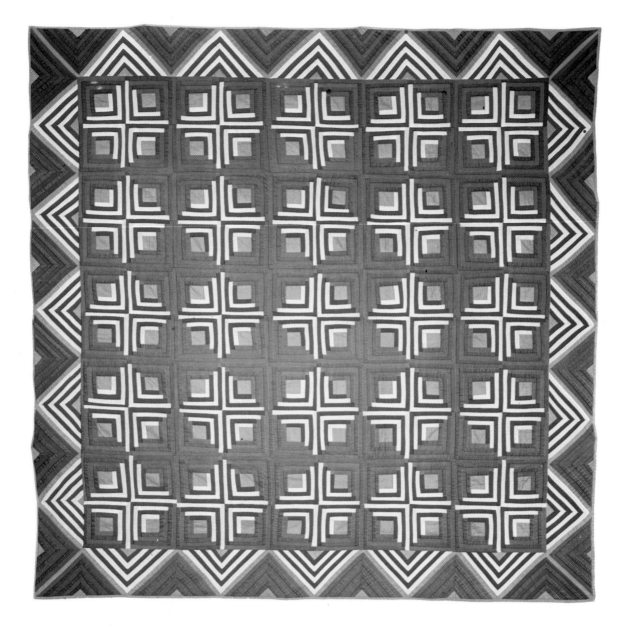

112. Pieced quilt, Log Cabin, Light and Dark design, c. 1885, Pennsylvania. 88″ x 87½″. The bright portions of this extraordinary quilt burn with an almost neon-light intensity. (America Hurrah Antiques, N.Y.C.)

Other examples of Log Cabin quilts are illustrated in plates 25, 32, 52, 61, 63, 69, 90, 94, 123, 125, 131, 167.

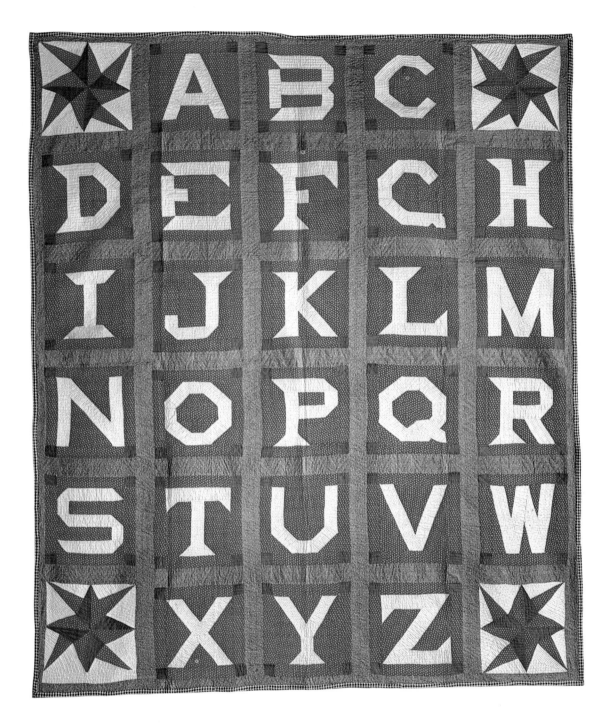

113. Pieced quilt, Alphabet, c. 1885, Pennsylvania. 89″ x 75″. One supposes that Alphabet quilts were specifically created for children. This is one of the most pleasing examples, for the squared-off shaping of the letters gives the feeling that they were constructed with children's blocks. (Thos. K. Woodard: American Antiques & Quilts)

114

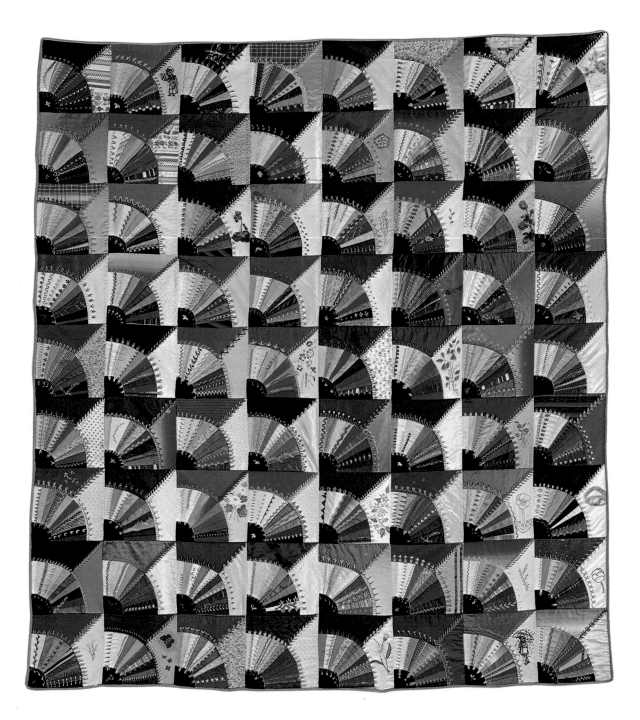

114. Pieced and embroidered quilt, Victorian Fans, silk, c. 1895. 61″ x 55″. This parlor throw is a particularly elegant example of the popular Fan design. The stitchery is widely varied—even to including some Chinese characters! (Thos. K. Woodard: American Antiques & Quilts)

115. Pieced and appliqué quilt, Album Basket, c. 1860, Pennsylvania. 88″ x 78″. The special delight of this piece is the variety of flora and fauna that perch atop the baskets. Note especially the three squares at the right edge that contain a weathercock between two houses, a pair of giraffes, and deer gamboling among trees. (America Hurrah Antiques, N.Y.C.)

Other examples of Album quilts are illustrated in plates 4, 7, 74, 80, 87, 147, 174.

116. Pieced quilt, Star of France, c. 1930. 79″ x 78″. In the 1982 calendar, where this lovely Star was first illustrated, I called this Desert Star because the desert colors gave a strong Southwest American Indian feeling to the quilt. Soon after the 1982 calendar was published I had the good fortune of hearing from Cuesta Benberry, a scholar in the field of American quilts, who was kind enough to let me know that the pattern for this Star was designed by H. Ver Mehren's Home Art Studio in Des Moines, Iowa, and it is called Star of France in his catalogue. The pattern is based on a Napoleonic medal. Photograph courtesy America Hurrah Antiques, N.Y.C. (Private collection)

Other examples of Star quilts are illustrated in plates 20, 22, 78, 79, 85, 106, 118, 129, 134, 143, 144, 152, 165, 170, 171, 178, 179, 185.

117. Pieced quilt, North Carolina Lily variation, 1900–1910, Mifflin County, Pennsylvania. 76″ x 75″. This charmer, which was created from home-dyed fabric, is based on one of the most familiar quilt patterns. However, the folk artist who made the quilt was obviously determined to use the motif in her own special way, and she succeeded beautifully. (Bettie Mintz: All of Us Americans Folk Art)

118. Pieced quilt, Star of Bethlehem, c. 1850, New England. 94½″ x 93″. This stunning quilt contains a total of 193 stars. Its maker obviously was determined to create her own personal galaxy! Photograph courtesy Thos. K. Woodard: American Antiques & Quilts. (Private collection)

Other examples of Star quilts are illustrated in plates 20, 22, 78, 79, 85, 106, 116, 129, 134, 143, 144, 152, 165, 170, 171, 178, 179, 185.

119. Crewel-embroidered wool coverlet, Medallion, 1815–1830, New England. 97" x 78". Compare this piece to that illustrated in plate 54 and the similarities in design and technique will be immediately apparent. What makes this rare coverlet particularly interesting is the use of a brown background instead of the more usual black. (The Henry Francis du Pont Winterthur Museum)

Other examples of Medallion quilts are illustrated in plates 1, 2, 3, 4, 13, 35, 36, 45, 49, 51, 54, 55, 57, 58, 70, 82, 83, 84, 99, 102, 106, 107, 108, 122, 127, 128, 138, 146, 159, 164, 175, 176, 183.

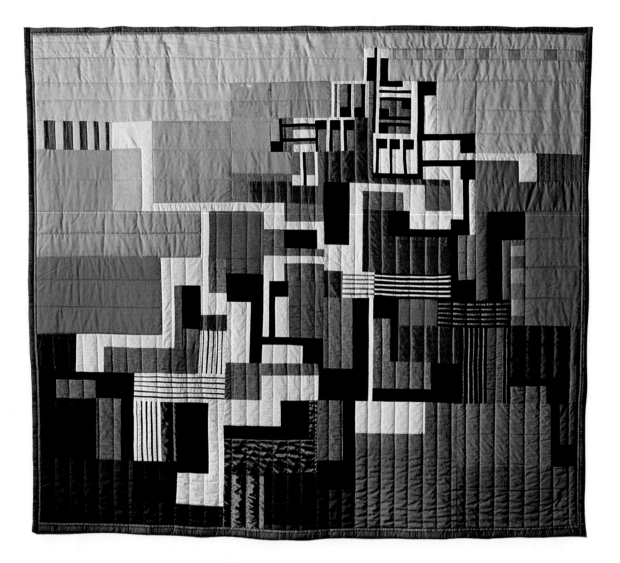

120. Quilted tapestry, *Note Motion*, made by Molly Upton, 1975, New York. 91″ x 104″. This splendid hanging shows how effectively quilting techniques have been used by a contemporary artist. Photograph courtesy Kornblee Gallery. (New Canaan Bank and Trust Company)

121. Pieced quilt, Triple Irish Chain, dated 1898 and inscribed "Manda and Glen Binkley," Ohio. 83″ x 71″. This is the most impressive Irish Chain I have seen. The architectural weight of the central panel is emphasized by the strong border and counterpointed by the fine quilting in the white reserves. Photograph courtesy Kiracofe and Kile. (Private collection)

122. Pieced *Hat and Hearts Wedding Quilt*, made in 1981 by Teresa Barkley for the marriage of Debra Ruth Marin and Joseph Zvi Lewanda, New York. 74″ x 74″. Made in the Medallion style, this charming quilt was inspired by the touching quilted valentine inscribed to "Squire Baldwine" illustrated in plate 95. In tribute to the quilter's New York origin the central square containing the hat and heart is framed with halves of four apples. Photograph courtesy the artist. (Collection of the artist)

Other examples of Medallion quilts are illustrated in plates 1, 2, 3, 4, 13, 35, 36, 45, 49, 51, 54, 55, 57, 58, 70, 82, 83, 84, 99, 102, 106, 107, 108, 119, 127, 128, 138, 146, 159, 164, 175, 176, 183.

123. Pieced quilt, Log Cabin variation, c. 1900. 80″ x 68″. Based on the Straight Furrow design, this startling, bold quilt has been made very contemporary by the addition of the black sashes, which compartmentalize the design, and by the segmented border. (Kelter-Malcé Antiques)

Other examples of Log Cabin quilts are illustrated in plates 25, 32, 52, 61, 63, 69, 90, 94, 112, 125, 131, 167.

124. Pieced quilt, Cross-in-the-Square/Center Diamond, wool, Amish, 1910–1920, Lancaster County, Pennsylvania. 83½″ x 83″. Not only are the colors beautiful in themselves, but they have also been expertly arranged to get the most impact from them. The large diamond composed of red blocks is, of course, a direct allusion to the classic Center Diamond style. Photograph courtesy Adirondack Memories. (Collection of Lois Stulberg)

Other examples of Amish Center Diamond quilts are illustrated in plates 6, 8, 66, 97, 126, 142, 154.

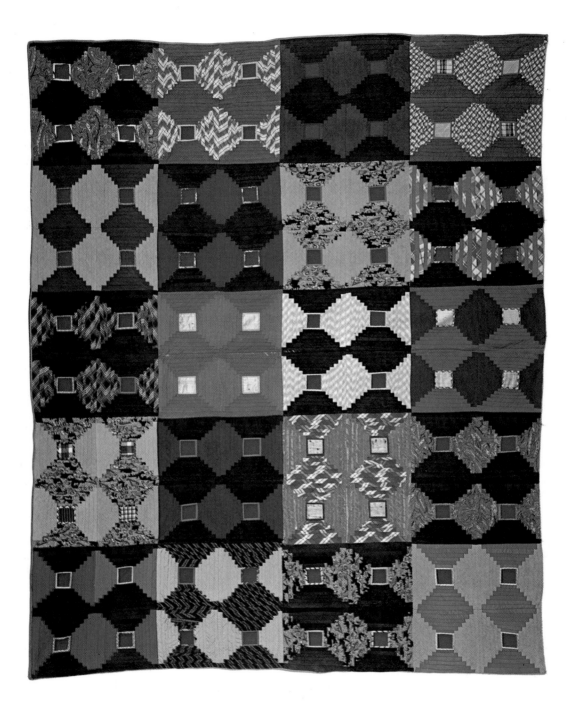

125. Pieced quilt, Log Cabin, Courthouse Steps design, wool challis, c. 1885, Pennsylvania. 78″ x 64″. Few Courthouse Steps quilts I have seen have the power and brilliance of color and pattern seen in this most unusual example. (Thos. K. Woodard: American Antiques & Quilts)

Other examples of Log Cabin quilts are illustrated in plates 25, 32, 52, 61, 63, 69, 90, 94, 112, 123, 131, 167.

126. Pieced quilt, Center Diamond, wool, Amish, c. 1900, Lancaster County, Pennsylvania. 80″ x 80″. The color in this piece is of such depth and brilliance it is almost mesmerizing. (America Hurrah Antiques, N.Y.C.)

Other examples of Amish Center Diamond quilts are illustrated in plates 6, 8, 66, 97, 124, 142, 154.

127. Appliqué quilt, *Cloister: Ascetic and Pious*, 1977, made in the Medallion style by Phyllis Varineau, Tucson, Arizona. 81″ x 81″. The designs in the border of this quilt were inspired by choral-book illustrations of c. 1750 at Ephrata Cloister, Ephrata, Pennsylvania. The bird in the center is a Schwenkfelder design of c. 1850. Photograph courtesy the artist. (Collection of the artist)

Other examples of Medallion quilts are illustrated in plates 1, 2, 3, 4, 13, 35, 36, 45, 49, 51, 54, 55, 57, 58, 70, 82, 83, 84, 99, 102, 106, 107, 108, 119, 122, 128,138, 146, 159, 164, 175, 176, 183.

128. Pieced and appliqué crib quilt, Medallion/Broderie Perse, 1830–1840, found in New York State. 34″ x 33½″. Early printed cottons are combined with delicate chintz cutouts in this elegant miniature. It was a privileged child indeed that was warmed by this beauty. Photograph courtesy Thos. K. Woodard: American Antiques & Quilts. (Private collection)

Other examples of Broderie Perse quilts are illustrated in plates 3, 99, 130, 145.

Other examples of crib quilts are illustrated in plates 16, 28, 65, 75, 111, 144, 150, 165.

Other examples of Medallion quilts are illustrated in plates 1, 2, 3, 4, 13, 35, 36, 45, 49, 51, 54, 55, 57, 58, 70, 82, 83, 84, 99, 102, 106, 107, 108, 119, 122, 127, 138, 146, 159, 164, 175, 176, 183.

129. Pieced and appliqué quilt, Feathered Star within Feathered Touching Stars, c. 1860. 98″ x 82″. The bold "trees" in the border make a strong frame for the handsome and intricate central design. Floral designs are also used in the quilting. Photograph courtesy America Hurrah Antiques, N.Y.C. (Private collection)

Other examples of Feathered Star quilts are illustrated in plates 100, 178.

Other examples of Touching Stars quilts are illustrated in plates 47, 56, 76, 156.

130. Pieced and appliqué quilt, Broderie Perse/Tree of Life, c. 1925, Wiscasset, Maine. 96″ x 90″. The tree in this lovely creation blossoms with birds and flowers made with fabrics from both the 1830s and the 1920s. The borders also have some contrasting prints interspersed in the designs. Photograph courtesy America Hurrah Antiques, N.Y.C. (Private collection)

Other examples of Broderie Perse quilts are illustrated in plates 3, 99, 128, 145.

Other examples of Tree of Life quilts are illustrated in plates 41, 46.

131. Pieced quilt, Log Cabin, Streak o' Lightning design, silk, c. 1865, New York State. 72″ x 66″. The sheen of the silk gives a special dimension to the softly modulated colors in this splendid Log Cabin. Note that the border has been made in the Courthouse Steps design. (America Hurrah Antiques, N.Y.C.)

Other examples of Log Cabin quilts are illustrated in plates 25, 32, 52, 61, 63, 69, 90, 94, 112, 123, 125, 167.

132. Pieced quilt, Bars, wool, Amish, 1895–1900, Lancaster County, Pennsylvania.
80″ x 80″. It would be hard to find another Amish Bars quilt with more beautiful
quilting or with a subtler palette than this example. Note how the circles of feather
quilting in the center are framed by an octagon. (America Hurrah Antiques, N.Y.C.)

Other examples of Amish Bars quilts are illustrated in plates 38, 91, 168.

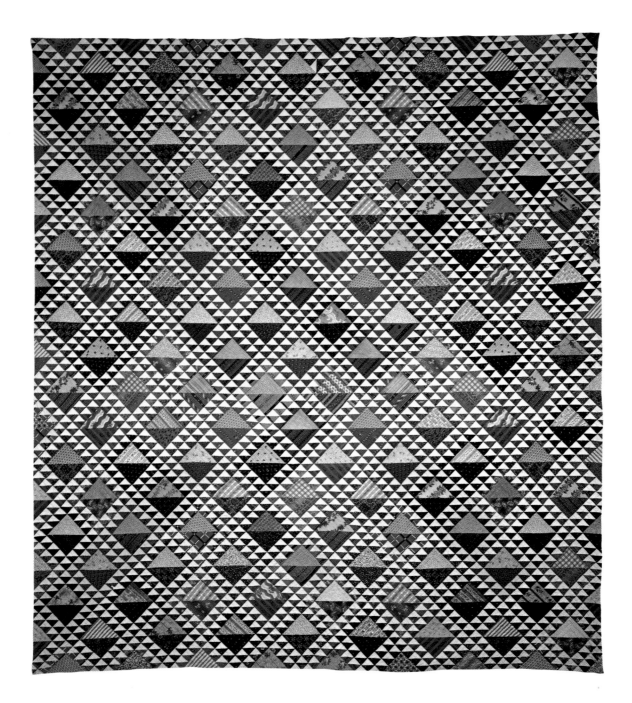

133. Pieced quilt, Lady of the Lake, c. 1840, New England. 106″ x 99″. Great color, great printed fabrics, and a forceful design of lights and darks make a very satisfying whole. (Thos. K. Woodard: American Antiques & Quilts)

134. Pieced quilt, Star of Bethlehem, c. 1880, New York State. 76″ x 80″. The spaces created by the points of the star lend themselves to a wide variety of design possibilities, as shown in this book. In this example the spaces are used most effectively to emphasize the importance of the central star, because all of the dark triangles are pointed toward it. (America Hurrah Antiques, N.Y.C.)

Other examples of Star quilts are illustrated in plates 20, 22, 78, 79, 85, 106, 116, 118, 143, 144, 152, 165, 170, 171, 178, 179, 185.

135. Pieced Triangles quilt, c. 1875, New York State. 86″ x 74″. This quilt is very similar in feeling to that in plate 49. Both rejoice in a collection of handsome calicoes artfully arranged in a satisfying composition of lights and darks. This example has a most interesting kaleidoscopic effect. (America Hurrah Antiques, N.Y.C.)

136. Pieced and appliqué quilt, Mariner's Compass, c. 1850. 94″ x 77″. The beauty
of the early fabrics is highlighted by the richness of the stuffed-work designs in the
background. Note the red heart placed in each of the four corners. (Thos. K.
Woodard: American Antiques & Quilts)

137. Appliqué quilt, Cherry Trees, 1880–1890, probably Midwest. 75¼" x 78½". The arching, berry-loaded branches and the floral swagged border give special zest to the red-and-green color scheme. (The Brick Store Museum; Gift of Mrs. Thomas W. Howard, 1963)

138. Appliqué quilt, Medallion, dated 1818, Rochester, New York. 84″ x 78″. This magnificent quilt, made sprightly with festoons, flowers, and birds all rendered in early printed cottons, is inscribed: "Done by Ann Daggs the 1 of May 1818." (America Hurrah Antiques, N.Y.C.)

Other examples of Medallion quilts are illustrated in plates 1, 2, 3, 4, 13, 35, 36, 45, 49, 51, 54, 55, 57, 58, 70, 82, 83, 84, 99, 102, 106, 107, 108, 119, 122, 127, 128, 146, 159, 164, 175, 176, 183.

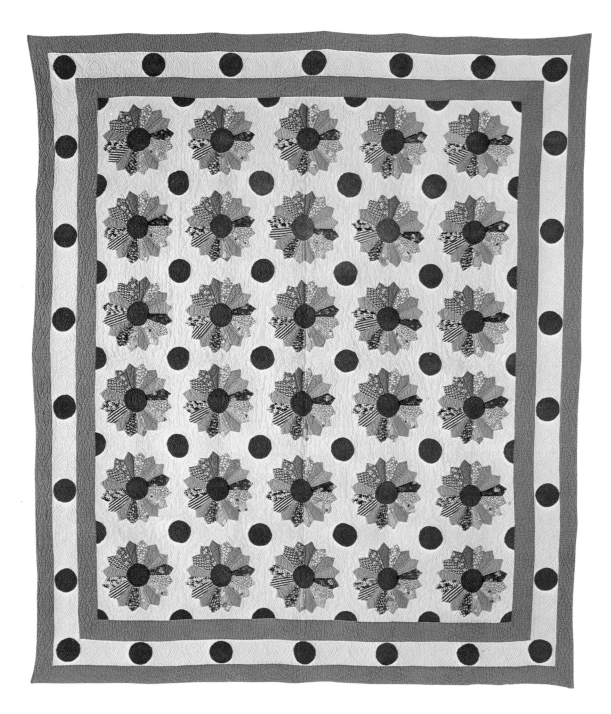

139. Pieced quilt, Dresden Plate, c. 1930. 84″ x 72″. Dresden Plate is one of the most popular of all quilt designs. In this example the large red circles give the piece a special graphic excitement. Note also that the same fabrics are used in each "plate" and are placed in the same positions throughout. (America Hurrah Antiques, N.Y.C.)

140. Pieced quilt, *Crazy City*, made by C. Winne, 1885, probably New York State. 82″ x 73″. Without any question this is the finest and most imaginative House quilt one could ever hope to find—a masterpiece that effervesces with color, design, and pattern.

Other examples of Crazy quilts are illustrated in plates 26, 31, 73, 89, 93.

Other examples of House quilts are illustrated in plates 14, 34, 46.

141. Pieced quilt, Chips and Whetstones, c. 1845, New England. 98″ x 76″. This is a prime example of the beauty that can be created from a bag of fabric scraps. The composition is unified by the blue-and-gold background in the squares, and against this is played the blue, brown, and rose tones of the scraps—with great success. (Thos. K. Woodard: American Antiques & Quilts)

142. Pieced quilt, Center Diamond, wool, Amish, c. 1900, Lancaster County, Pennsylvania. 78″ x 76″. The crimson center of this piece is so strongly set off by the bright blue triangles that it appears almost to pulsate. (Thos. K. Woodard: American Antiques & Quilts)

Other examples of Amish Center Diamond quilts are illustrated in plates 6, 8, 66, 97, 124, 126, 154.

143. Pieced quilt, Broken Star, c. 1920, Mifflin County, Pennsylvania. 85¼″ x 76″.
Here is one of the most fascinating of the Star patterns, for it makes it possible for
the artist to create a quilt that seems to explode with colorful energy—in this case
both well framed and contained by the black background. (Kelter-Malcé
Antiques)

Other examples of Star quilts are illustrated in plates 20, 22, 78, 79, 85, 106, 116, 118,
129, 134, 144, 152, 165, 170, 171, 178, 179, 185.

144. Pieced and appliqué crib quilt, Star of Bethlehem with Variable Star border, c. 1840, New England. 45¼" x 45½". It would be hard to find a more beautiful miniature Star of Bethlehem than this, for it is alive with color and pattern. The Pot of Flowers motifs between the star's points are especially charming. (George E. Schoellkopf Gallery)

Other examples of crib quilts are illustrated in plates 16, 28, 65, 75, 111, 128, 150, 165.

Other examples of Star quilts are illustrated in plates 20, 22, 78, 79, 85, 106, 116, 118, 129, 134, 143, 152, 165, 170, 171, 178, 179, 185.

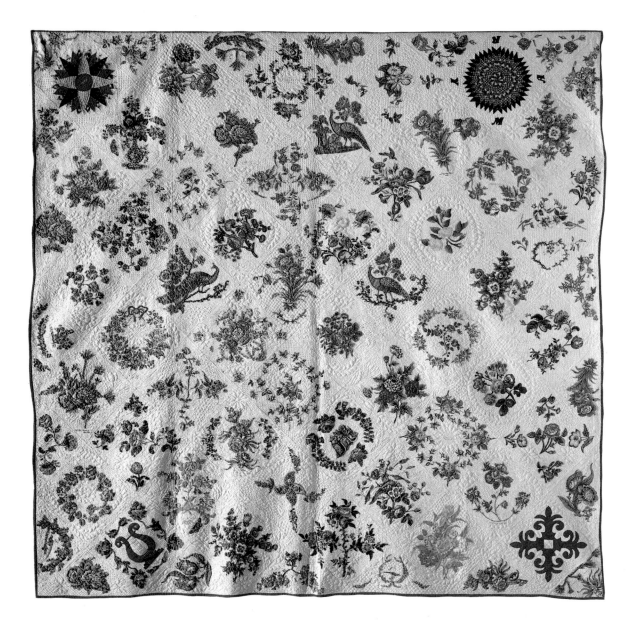

145. Pieced and appliqué quilt, Broderie Perse, 1835–1846, Massillon, Stark County, Ohio. 92″ x 96″. Isabel Hall Hurxthal, the wife of Louis Hurxthal, one of the founders of Massillon, was the maker of this very beautiful quilt with its great and varied collection of appliquéd cutouts from French chintz. Many of the squares bear the autographs of friends and relatives, and the whole is noteworthy for its delicacy and refinement, emphasized by the exquisite quilting surrounding the cutouts. (The Massillon Museum)

146. Appliqué quilt with stuffed-work designs, Medallion, c. 1840, possibly New England. 92″ x 78″. This masterpiece incorporates elements of stuffed work not only on the front but on the back as well, for the quilt is completely reversible. At the bottom left of the central bouquet (neatly tied with a ribbon) is an equestrian statue of Henry Clay, and George Washington can be seen riding a horse to the right of the central design. (America Hurrah Antiques, N.Y.C.)

Other examples of quilts with stuffed work are illustrated in plates 3, 10, 12, 58, 74, 99, 100, 180.

Other examples of Medallion quilts are illustrated in plates 1, 2, 3, 4, 13, 35, 36, 45, 49, 51, 54, 55, 57, 58, 70, 82, 83, 84, 99, 102, 106, 107, 108, 119, 122, 127, 128, 138, 159, 164, 175, 176, 183.

147. Pieced and appliqué quilt, Album, c. 1850, Baltimore, Maryland. 117″ x 117″. Judging from the red-and-green color scheme and the fact that holly is featured in the center of the top row, it would appear that this very handsome Baltimore Album quilt was intended as a Christmas gift. Photograph courtesy Thos. K. Woodard: American Antiques & Quilts. (Cora Ginsburg)

Other examples of Album quilts are illustrated in plates, 4, 7, 14, 80, 87, 115, 174.

148. Pieced quilt, Mariner's Compass with appliqué, 1855–1865, New England. 89½″ x 75½″. It is the slivers of white in the compass motifs that give real sparkle to this quilt, and the alternating red and green leaf forms give a delightful rhythm to the border. (America Hurrah Antiques, N.Y.C.)

149. Appliqué quilt, Pot of Flowers, c. 1870, Ohio. 92″ x 87″. Because red and green was probably the favorite color combination with which to create floral appliqués one always looks forward to seeing unusual quilts using these colors. Here is a particularly graceful example of the type, and the quilting of the background is especially fine. Photograph courtesy Kelter-Malcé Antiques. (Private collection)

Other examples of Pot of Flowers quilts are illustrated in plates 15, 20, 21, 60, 157, 173, 181.

150. Appliqué crib quilt, Princess Feather, c. 1895. 44″ x 44″. It may be small, but it packs a wallop! The creator of this miniature obviously wished to make a bright and bold statement. Photograph courtesy America Hurrah Antiques, N.Y.C. (Private collection)

Other examples of crib quilts are illustrated in plates 16, 28, 65, 75, 111, 128, 144, 165.

151. Pieced quilt, Sampler, Amish, c. 1920, Ohio. 80″ x 68″. The splashy color and bold motifs are what one finds so enticing in this quilt. Its creator obviously decided she wanted to prove her skill with many designs, and the result is an impressive "duke's mixture." (Kelter-Malcé Antiques)

152. Pieced quilt, Feathered Star variation, c. 1920, Ohio. 74" x 70". Appropriate to all patriotic occasions, this is a very zippy use of red, white, and blue. It takes high honors for graphic excitement. (America Hurrah Antiques, N.Y.C.)

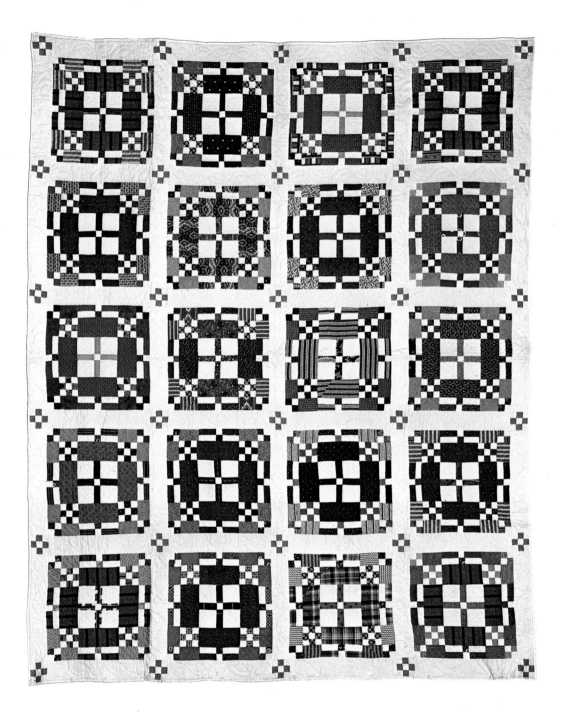

153. Pieced quilt, Road to California, c. 1875, Pennsylvania. 90″ x 72″. It is a delightful name for a beautiful quilt, but one does wonder how the name originated. The quilt contains a fine collection of brown calicoes. (America Hurrah Antiques, N.Y.C.)

154. Pieced quilt, Center Diamond, wool, Amish, c. 1900, Lancaster County, Pennsylvania. 82″ x 82″. The expertly modulated color in this quilt wraps one in warmth and beauty just like fire on a hearth. (America Hurrah Antiques, N.Y.C.)

Other examples of Amish Center Diamond quilts are illustrated in plates 6, 8, 66, 97, 124, 126, 142.

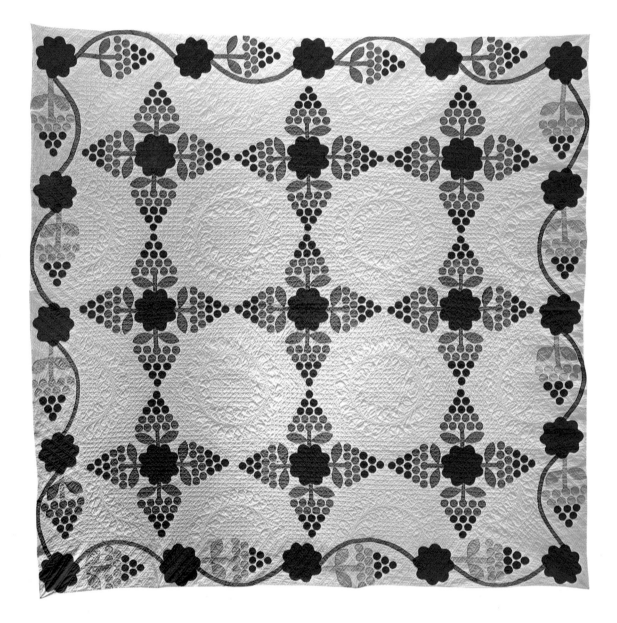

155. Appliqué quilt, Flowers and Grapes, c. 1900, Pennsylvania. 85″ x 83″. Bold color, bold design, and fine quilting make this a winner. Note how the color of the top portion of the lowest bunch of grapes in the left border appears to have been piously and deliberately changed from tan to blue to avoid perfection. (Kelter-Malcé Antiques)

156. Pieced and appliqué quilt, Touching Stars with Delectable Mountains border, c. 1870, Pennsylvania. 90″ x 89″. The red-and-green elements in this quilt provide a strong counterpoint to the bold stars. (Kelter-Malcé Antiques)

Other examples of Touching Stars quilts are illustrated in plates 47, 56, 76, 129.

157. Stencil spread, Pot of Flowers, 1825–1835, New England. 91″ x 84″. Fine stencil spreads are a rarity, and this is a particularly beautiful example. Note the tiny birds perching among the flowers. The motifs were created by applying paint to the background cloth through patterns cut in heavy paper. (Museum of American Folk Art; Gift of George E. Schoellkopf)

Other examples of stencil spreads are illustrated in plates 175, 176.

Other examples of Pot of Flowers quilts are illustrated in plates 15, 20, 21, 60, 149, 173, 181.

158. Pieced and appliqué quilt, Stars and Blossoms, c. 1870, Pennsylvania. 88″ x 88″. Because of the rich brown of the background the motifs in this quilt give the appearance of having sprung from the Pennsylvania soil. (Thos. K. Woodard: American Antiques & Quilts)

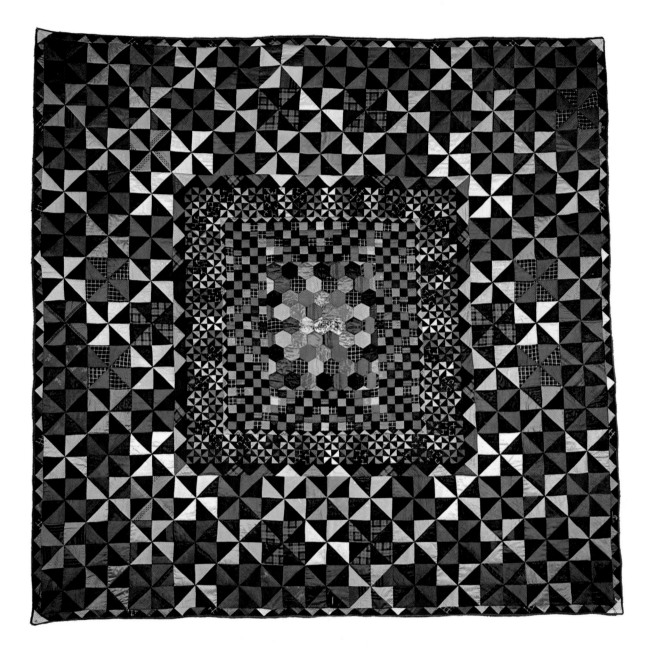

159. Pieced quilt, Medallion with borders in Pinwheel design, silk, 1850–1860. 84″ x 84″. In this rich tapestry of color note how the direction of the pinwheels has been reversed in the inner border to emphasize the sense of motion. (America Hurrah Antiques, N.Y.C.)

Other examples of Medallion quilts are illustrated in plates 1, 2, 3, 4, 13, 35, 36, 45, 49, 51, 54, 55, 57, 58, 70, 82, 83, 84, 99, 102, 106, 107, 108, 119, 122, 127, 128, 138, 146, 164, 175, 176, 183.

160. Appliqué quilt, Trees and Garlands, c. 1930, Pennsylvania. 94″ x 78″. It is probable that all the elements in this 1930s quilt with its very stylish Lombardy poplars were purchased in a kit for assembly at home. The quilting, which echoes the tree design, would have been prestamped on the cloth. The result is handsome indeed. (Thos. K. Woodard: American Antiques & Quilts)

161. Pieced and appliqué quilt, Whig Rose variation, c. 1855, New England. 71¾″ x 69½″. The four large floral motifs seem to explode like rockets against the white background, and the touches of golden yellow give special zest to the familiar red-and-green color scheme. (America Hurrah Antiques, N.Y.C.)

162. Appliqué quilt, unique design, inscribed "Made by Mrs. D. Van Voorhis, aged 7 [?] 1865," Pennsylvania. 103″ x 88″. Another equally unusual quilt by this artist, employing two of the same designs, is illustrated in *America's Quilts and Coverlets*. The motifs in this piece, with the exception of the cactus plants, appear to have a very personal meaning. Photograph courtesy Thos. K. Woodard: American Antiques & Quilts. (Private collection)

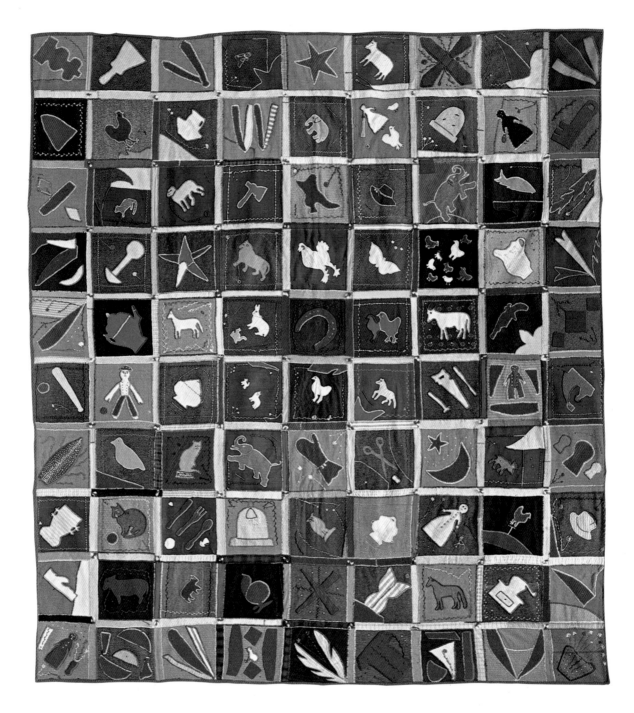

163. Appliqué quilt, wool, c. 1890, Kentucky. 93″ x 82″. The wonderful images in this quilt give it an almost picturebook quality; surely it was created to delight a child. (Thos. K. Woodard: American Antiques & Quilts)

164. Pieced quilt, Medallion, 1880–1890, Maine. 87½″ x 82¾″. The nautical theme of this stunning quilt, which was inspired by a compass rose, is enhanced by the blue calico that has a design of white anchors. The central design appears to be a variation of the Princess Feather design. Photograph courtesy Cora Ginsburg. (Museum of American Folk Art)

Other examples of Medallion quilts are illustrated in plates 1, 2, 3, 4, 13, 35, 36, 45, 49, 51, 54, 55, 57, 58, 70, 82, 83, 84, 99, 102, 106, 107, 108, 119, 122, 127, 128, 138, 146, 159, 175, 176, 183.

165. Pieced crib quilt, Le Moyne Star, 1840–1850. 40½″ x 37½″. The simplest of designs derives added interest from the early fabrics with which it is made. Photograph George E. Schoellkopf Gallery. (Private collection)

Other examples of crib quilts are illustrated in plates 16, 28, 65, 75, 111, 128, 144, 150.

Other examples of Star quilts are illustrated in plates 20, 22, 78, 79, 85, 106, 116, 118, 129, 134, 143, 144, 152, 170, 171, 178, 179, 185.

166. Appliqué quilt, *Noah's Landing*, designed and made in 1974 by Dorothy and Abby Brooks, Pennsylvania. 95″ x 75″. The Ark has arrived safely, and the many travelers are stretching themselves and inspecting the new territory. This is a splendid interpretation of the biblical tale. Photograph courtesy the artists. (Collection of Abby Brooks)

Other examples of pictorial appliqué quilts are illustrated in plates 30, 50, 64, 67, 81, 169.

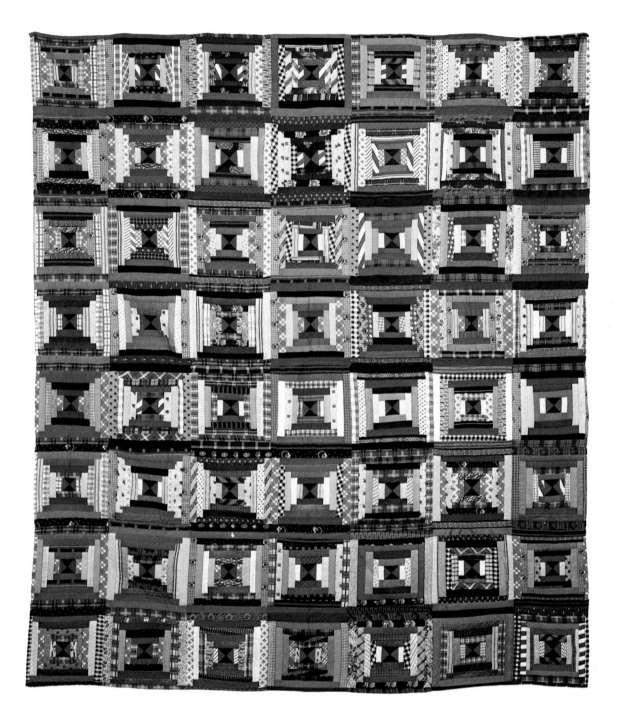

167. Pieced quilt, Log Cabin, Courthouse Steps design, Mennonite, c. 1875, Pennsylvania. 68" x 60". The bright colors and patterns and liberal use of white make this quilt sparkle. (America Hurrah Antiques, N.Y.C.)

Other examples of Log Cabin quilts are illustrated in plates 25, 32, 52, 61, 63, 69, 90, 94, 112, 123, 125, 131.

168. Pieced quilt, Split Bars, wool, Amish, c. 1925, Lancaster County, Pennsylvania. 82″ x 78″. The Amish continually astound us with their very sophisticated use of color, as in this extraordinary example. (America Hurrah Antiques, N.Y.C.)

Other examples of Amish Bars quilts are illustrated in plates 38, 91, 132.

169. Appliqué quilt, made by Mrs. Cecil White, c. 1930, Hartford, Connecticut. 77″ x 66″. Mrs. White created a major example of American folk art in the quilt medium, for its many vignettes are fascinating and amusing glimpses of everyday life. Photograph courtesy Rhea Goodman. (Private collection)

Other examples of pictorial appliqué quilts are illustrated in plates 30, 50, 64, 67, 81, 166.

170. Pieced quilt, Star Burst, c. 1940, Michigan. 82″ x 66″. This book contains Star quilts of every possible type—almost—yet none of them has quite the pop, sizzle, and flash of this one. (Wild Goose Chase Quilt Gallery)

Other examples of Star quilts are illustrated in plates 20, 22, 78, 79, 85, 106, 116, 118, 129, 134, 143, 144, 152, 165, 171, 178, 179, 185.

171. Pieced quilt, Lone Star, c. 1930. 90″ x 90″. Handsomely quilted, this Star features the color called "Tango," which was very fashionable at the time the quilt was made. Photograph courtesy Thos. K. Woodard: American Antiques & Quilts. (Private collection)

Other examples of Star quilts are illustrated in plates 20, 22, 78, 79, 85, 106, 116, 118, 129, 134, 143, 144, 152, 165, 170, 178, 179, 185.

172. Pieced quilt, Union Square, wool, Amish, c. 1920, Geauga County, Ohio. 92″ x 78″. This quilt achieves the glowing beauty of stained glass, but through textiles. (Darwin D. Bearley)

Other examples of Midwestern Amish quilts are illustrated on pages 2–3 and in plates 5, 23, 41, 62.

173. Pieced and appliqué quilt, Pot of Flowers, c. 1930. 88″ x 82″. The art of quilting enjoyed a true renascence in the 1930s, and this is one of the finest examples I have seen from that period. It was quite possibly created with commercial patterns. (Thos. K. Woodard: American Antiques & Quilts)

Other examples of Pot of Flowers quilts are illustrated in plates 15, 20, 21, 60, 149, 157, 181.

174. Pieced and appliqué quilt, Album, c. 1855, New York State. 87¾″ x 69¼″.
Originally published in the 1975 calendar, this *jeu d'esprit* might aptly be called
Lollipop Trees. I have yet to see another quilt that can match its delightful whimsy.
(America Hurrah Antiques, N.Y.C.)

Other examples of Album quilts are illustrated in plates 4, 7, 74, 80, 87, 115, 147.

175. Stenciled and printed spread, *Yard Quilt*, designed and made in the Medallion style by Margot Strand Jensen, 1979, Riner, Virginia. 78″ x 64″. The artist has used the classic techniques of stenciling, block printing, piecing, and quilting to make a beautiful and lively contemporary quilt. Photograph courtesy the artist. (Collection of the artist)

Other examples of stencil spreads are illustrated in plates 157, 176.

Other examples of Medallion quilts are illustrated in plates 1, 2, 3, 4, 13, 35, 36, 45, 49, 51, 54, 55, 57, 58, 70, 82, 83, 84, 99, 102, 106, 107, 108, 119, 122, 127, 128, 138, 146, 159, 164, 176, 183.

176. Stencil spread, Medallion, c. 1825, probably New England. 90″ x 89½″. This very elaborate piece reflects the somewhat heavy motifs of the Empire style that was fashionable when the spread was made. It is inscribed "Mrs. Sarah Mooers." Photograph courtesy Sotheby Parke Bernet, Inc. (Thos. K. Woodard: American Antiques & Quilts)

Other examples of stencil spreads are illustrated in plates 157, 175.

Other examples of Medallion quilts are illustrated in plates 1, 2, 3, 4, 13, 35, 36, 45, 49, 51, 54, 55, 57, 58, 70, 82, 83, 84, 99, 102, 106, 107, 108, 119, 122, 127, 128, 138, 146, 159, 164, 175, 183.

177. Pieced quilt, Pine Trees, c. 1930. 88″ x 70″. Bold, snappy prints and plaids from the Art Deco period decorate this grove of trees, which stands against the crisp white background of the quilt as if seen in a snowy landscape. Photograph courtesy Thos. K. Woodard: American Antiques & Quilts. (Private collection)

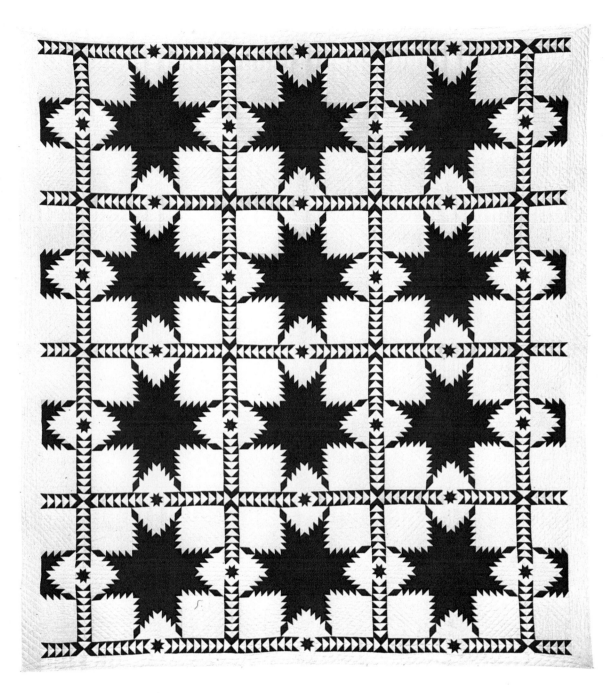

178. Pieced quilt, Feathered Star with Flying Geese sashes, c. 1860. 80½" x 71". Instead of containing her handsome stars within a framing border the artist has finished off the quilt at the left and right with small sections of the stars and sashes to give the illusion of their stretching into infinity. Photograph courtesy Rhea Goodman. (Private collection)

Other examples of Feathered Star quilts are illustrated in plates 100, 129.

Other examples of Star quilts are illustrated in plates 20, 22, 78, 79, 85, 106, 116, 118, 129, 134, 143, 144, 152, 165, 170, 171, 179, 185.

179. Pieced quilt, Star of Bethlehem, c. 1870, Massachusetts. 84″ x 87″. The special fascination of this quilt is, of course, the way in which the red-and-white triangles appear to enclose the star as if it were being wrapped in a large piece of cloth. (Kelter-Malcé Antiques)

Other examples of Star quilts are illustrated in plates 20, 22, 78, 79, 85, 106, 116, 118, 129, 134, 143, 144, 152, 165, 170, 171, 178, 185.

180. Pieced and appliqué quilt, North Carolina Lily variation, c. 1850. 80″ x 81″. This familiar pattern has sprouted a few more blossoms just to keep things interesting and to provide the extra visual weight to balance the marvelous floral stuffed work. The serpentine stuffed-work border in the Feather pattern adds the final touch of elegance. (Thos. K. Woodard: American Antiques & Quilts)

Other examples of quilts with stuffed work are illustrated in plates 3, 10, 12, 58, 74, 99, 100, 146.

181. Pieced and appliqué quilt, Pot of Flowers, c. 1870, Pennsylvania. 100¾″ x 73½″. Fourteen pots of red-and-blue calico contain bright flowers, fruit, and nine little birds. The way in which the pots have been set at different angles and the random elements used in the border between the pieced stars give the quilt a charming, unstudied effect, rather as if one were walking in a garden. The quilting is done in a flower-and-leaf design. (Private collection)

Other examples of Pot of Flowers quilts are illustrated in plates 15, 20, 21, 60, 149, 157, 173.

182. Pieced and appliqué quilt, Pineapple, 1860–1870, New Jersey. 88″ x 70″. Since the pineapple is the great symbol of hospitality, it seems probable that this quilt with its sprightly fruit was used to honor guests. (Thos. K. Woodard: American Antiques & Quilts)

183. Pieced quilt, Medallion with borders of Birds in the Air, c. 1895, New Jersey. 82″ x 74″. Here is dedicated planning and piecing! The broad bands containing thousands of triangles are effectively framed with narrow borders of triangles and zigzags. It all adds up to a brilliant work of art with great color and motion. Photograph courtesy America Hurrah Antiques, N.Y.C. (Private collection)

Other examples of Medallion quilts are illustrated in plates 1, 2, 3, 4, 13, 35, 36, 45, 49, 51, 54, 55, 57, 58, 70, 82, 83, 84, 99, 102, 106, 107, 108, 119, 122, 127, 128, 138, 146, 159, 164, 175, 176.

184. Pieced and appliqué quilt, North Carolina Lily with Le Moyne Star, c. 1855, New York State. 86″ x 78″. The very fine quilting of the background, the strong, vibrant color, and the tiny stars punctuating the space between the large motifs— all are combined into a superior example of American quilting. (America Hurrah Antiques, N.Y.C.)

185. Pieced quilt, Star of Bethlehem, c. 1900, Pennsylvania. 82″ x 82″. The boldly striped background obviously has been pieced so as to create the illusion that the great star is spinning—and spin it does in celebration of all the beauty, creativity, and proud accomplishment that have preceded it! (Kelter-Malcé Antiques)

Other examples of Star quilts are illustrated in plates 20, 22, 78, 79, 85, 106, 116, 118, 129, 134, 143, 144, 152, 165, 170, 171, 178, 179.

PATTERNS AND INSTRUCTIONS
FOR
MAKING YOUR OWN QUILTS

PATTERNS AND INSTRUCTIONS
FOR
MAKING YOUR OWN QUILTS

BE PREPARED—TO MAKE A QUILT

A quilt is a work of art, and as with a painting or a sculpture, it requires hours of planning and preparation. There are many incomplete quilts lying in attics; quite a few of them suffered from poor planning and were cast aside. Designing, color coordinating, and shopping can take days, and then there's still the second stage of testing fabrics, patterns, and your ability to make sure that you can see the project through.

Even when copying an antique quilt from an exact pattern, you will have to make many decisions, especially concerning fabrics which cannot be duplicated. Except in the case of the relatively few silk, wool, or velvet quilts, you can be sure that the original was 100% cotton. If you stay with the pure cottons now available, you will be more apt to achieve the soft colors and lovely texture of days gone by than if you work with the blends which have a high percentage of synthetic fiber. Many quilters find the 100% cottons easier to work with as well as more rewarding in appearance. Remember that the quilt you're copying is a priceless heirloom and the one you're making can be viewed with the same awe and respect a hundred years from now. Always think of your planning time as an investment in the future.

If you change the arrangement of colors from the quilt as illustrated, you will, of course, have to figure new yardages. If you make a larger or a smaller quilt from the block pattern given, the estimates will also have to be reworked. Help in doing this is usually available at quilt and/or fabric shops. It is better to have too much fabric than too little because patterns and dye lots change from season to season. Fabric leftovers can also spur quilters on to future projects.

One other factor may create problems in yardage estimates: the width from selvage to selvage. The requirements given here—and in most other books—are based on 45-inch cottons. There are some very beautiful English fabrics available that are only 36 inches wide, some European ones that are 39 inches, and a few meant for draperies that are 54 inches.

Once the fabrics have been selected, they must be washed to prevent future uneven shrinkage. Washing also takes out chemical finishes so that the fabric is softer and easier to handle. If you have any doubts about dark-colored fabrics running or bleeding, lay them on a white towel when they're wet. If no dark stain shows, they are safe. If they bleed, you have two choices: either replace them with other fabrics or soak them in a solution of three parts cold water and one part white vinegar, then rinse and test again. When the fabrics are wet, look at the reverse side to see whether or not the grain is straight. If it isn't, pull the fabric to line up the weave. Press the fabric just before it is dry, holding the grain square as you do so.

The proper choice of batting may be even more puzzling than that of fabric. There are new types on the market almost every year. Continual research and discussion are necessary if a quilter is to keep abreast of the various choices. Pure cotton batting or cotton with a small polyester content will make a quilt that looks more like those of the nineteenth or early twentieth century than will the new high-loft, all-synthetic types.

The backing should be compatible with the fabric chosen for the quilt top. Some quilters have used bed sheets because they afford a seamless backing. The general consensus is that it is hard to push a needle through heavily treated part-synthetic, no-iron sheets. Some 100% cotton sheets can be washed several times until they are quite soft and easy to use. In general, the backing should be made of two panels of 45-inch fabric seamed along the center, thus giving a wider range of fabric and color choices.

Needles, thread, and frames complete the list of supplies about which many choices have to be made. Thread, like fabric, requires much testing. Each quilter must make her own decision, and discussions of thread go on ad infinitum when quilters meet. It is safe to say that 100% cotton thread will work well with cotton fabric, and that any thread must be of a high quality with a good smooth finish.

Each quilter also has definite opinions about the best type of needle to use, some part of which is based on individual patience and eyesight. The tiny "quilting" or "between" needles are the most popular, but even in those there is a variation of size. Perfect eyesight and the desire to make the world's smallest stitches will sometimes prompt a quilter to use a size 10. A little less ambition will allow for anything down to size 7. A thimble becomes a real necessity with such tiny needles and so many stitches.

To use a quilting frame or not to use a frame is another lively topic of discussion. We have for so long pictured ladies sitting around a frame of dining-table size, quilting and gossiping, that it may come as a surprise to some to learn that quilting can be done totally alone and without so much as a lap frame. The important step is basting, although there is one fine old-fashioned way of putting a quilt in a frame without a single basting stitch. For the sake of simplicity the directions in this book stay with the basted methods.

The frame you choose will depend somewhat on the size of the area in which you plan to quilt, or whether or not you wish to be completely mobile, in which case you may resort to "lap quilting" without a frame. There are also small frames and hoops which can be hand held and carried from place to place. Look at frames, peruse catalogues, and discuss your problem with quilting friends and/or instructors before making a final decision about what will work best for you.

MAKING AND USING PATTERNS

Patterns for quilts, both pieced and appliquéd, are given in this book *without seam allowances* to assure complete accuracy. The exact-size patterns allow tracing around on the seamline so that stitching may be done easily and so that any width seam may be added, depending on the type of fabric, and size of the pieces. The general rule is to use a ¼-inch seam allowance for piecing patterns and slightly less for appliqué. Firmly woven cottons cut into very small pieces, such as those in the Mariner's Compass, p.197, may have slightly

smaller seam allowances. Test the fabric to see that it does not pull apart with a ⅛-inch seam. Any seam measuring less than ⅛ inch is too dangerous to try.

Patterns should be traced onto firm cardboard, stencil paper, or fine hard plastic. These are called templates. Use a ruler, a French curve, and a sharp pencil for accuracy. Cut with very sharp scissors or an X-acto knife. Some quilters like to cut their templates from a very fine sandpaper or to glue sandpaper onto any other material used. The rough surface of the sandpaper helps to hold the pattern in place on the fabric.

If you are uncertain of your ability to judge the width of the seam allowance accurately when cutting, you may want to make a second set of patterns or templates with the seam allowance added. Lay these on the wrong side of the fabric and draw around them with a medium pencil. Then lay the other templates inside the first markings and draw again. You now have cutting lines and stitching lines accurately marked.

If you use only the smaller templates, be sure to leave enough space between each marking to allow for seams (½ inch between allows for two ¼-inch seams). When laying any templates on the fabric, be aware of the grain lines so that at least one edge of any geometric piece is straight. The general rule is that the longest side of any triangle should be on the straight grain. You may have reasons for wanting to break this rule—to make plaids and stripes perform in a certain way in the design or so that a long bias edge will be stabilized by a long straight edge. Grain lines are marked on the pieces as a suggestion only. The one sure rule is that all four sides of any square or rectangular piece should be on the straight grain.

Patterns for the actual quilting can be made in several ways. (There will be more about marking the quilting designs in a later section.) The usual methods are: marking around a template with a hard pencil or water-soluble marker, tracing from a line drawing over a light box with pencil or marker, or using a punched paper or tin pattern and powdered chalk. For the last method you would use patterns already made up and sold by quilt suppliers.

For the first system you can make up templates as previously described—the thinner and harder the material the better. For the tracing method you must first trace the pattern with pen or dark pencil onto firm white paper. Next, place the paper on a light box or against a window pane, then lay the fabric over it and trace lightly. Taping the fabric to the glass helps to hold it in place as you work.

A simple light box can be made by suspending a pane of heavy glass between two piles of books—about 3 or 4 inches high—and laying a very small light bulb on a cord under it. Working on a window pane is pretty tiring if you're marking more than one small block.

When you have made all of the patterns for one quilt, punch holes in them and string them together. As all quilters know, small pieces have a bad habit of vanishing and then reappearing only after you have taken time out to remake them.

PIECING THE GEOMETRIC PATTERNS

All of those lovely Four Patch, Nine Patch, Star, and Compass patterns are made up of little geometric sections, seamed or pieced together *with great accuracy* so that they can then be organized into blocks of exact sizes. Carelessness and lack of attention to marked seam allowances will result in sure disaster. The greater the number of pieces in the block pattern, the greater the opportunity for going astray, so beginners should beware and choose a simple design such as the Amish Double Nine Patch, p. 217, or the Old Maid's Ramble, p. 234.

As the pieces are marked and cut, you will find that it helps to organize them into packets—ordinary plastic kitchen bags are fine—so that you can reach them easily. Starting with Old Maid's Ramble, which is a nice simple Four Patch, put all of the red #1 pieces in a bag, all of the white #2 together, red #3 together, and white #3 together. You can then reach for the next piece you want without searching. Notice that the grain lines as marked will allow most of the bias edges to be held firm by straight edges.

A Four Patch is always assembled by first sewing together the small pieces that form the four squares. Then two squares are sewn together to make one half of the block, then the two halves are joined. A Nine Patch is worked by first assembling nine squares, then three strips, and so forth. These divisions of the blocks are usually referred to as units.

Seams are made as in any other sewing by placing the right sides of the fabric together, matching and pinning the seamline, and then stitching. The greatest accuracy

is achieved by pinning at right angles to the seamline, taking up only a small amount of fabric right on the seamline. Pin at each end of the seam first, then at intervals between.

When joining seams by hand, use a small even running stitch. Start with a firm, neat knot and a backstitch. On long seams put in a small backstitch at intervals to secure the stitching. Fasten off at the end with two backstitches, running the thread through the loop of the last stitch before pulling it tight. Press each seam to one side, preferably toward the darker fabric, before sewing another seam across it. Be especially sure to press each unit as it is finished, then each block as it is finished.

Seams may be joined by machine. Start by pinning in exactly the same way as for hand sewing; modern machines are equipped to sew across pins set perpendicular to the seamline. Adjust the machine so that the tension is smooth and there are ten to twelve stitches to the inch. It is possible to line up a number of pieces and sew directly from one to the next until they are all

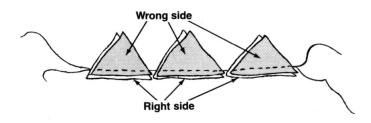

hanging on a long string together, then cut them apart. This assembly-line method saves considerable time.

In more difficult patterns such as the Mariner's Compass, p. 197, it is almost impossible to join the pieces by machine. When working by hand, it will be necessary at certain V points to stop the stitching at the seam intersection and fasten off, leaving in effect a clip

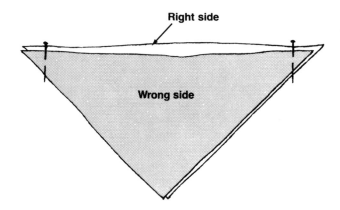

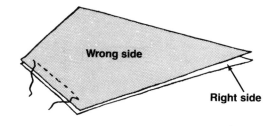

that can be bent back to allow the next piece to be seamed in, one side at a time.

The other difficulty in piecing is the joining of curved seams. A concave curve is always joined to a convex and they react somewhat differently. Working exactly on the seamline to make them fit together is even more important than with straight seams. Again, pinning at the ends first will help to ensure a neat joining. It is sometimes necessary to stretch the concave line slightly to make it fit around the convex. If all else fails, clip along the concave line at intervals, but not too deeply.

After all the blocks are made and pressed, set them together in rows, with sashes between if they are called for. Press again and join the rows together, being sure that all of the blocks line up squarely. Make up and add on the borders. Now you are ready to assemble the layered quilt.

APPLIQUÉ

Quilters find that appliqué gives an even wider scope to the imagination than the precise patterns of piecing. The technique is simple, and almost anything that can be sketched on paper can be more or less reproduced in appliqué, which is the application of cut-out pieces of fabric to a base fabric.

Several forms of appliqué design are favored by quilters. One of the oldest employs motifs printed on chintz or other cotton fabrics—birds, fruits, and trees—cut out and rearranged onto a plain background. These are often seen in Medallion quilts, sometimes mixed with pieced or solid borders, p. viii. Another type of design, used especially in Hawaii and Pennsylvania, is what can be called paperfold, a technique that is rather like making snowflakes in kindergarten (see Double Hearts, p. 253). The third method is to draw freehand or trace simple shapes from coloring books, around actual leaves from trees, found objects, or shadows.

There are two ways of preparing appliqué for the actual stitching, which should always be done with a tiny blind stitch as nearly invisible as possible. The way in which most beginners learn is more suited to the simpler shapes.

First method: Trace the pattern on the wrong side of the decorative fabric. Leave an allowance of slightly less than ¼ inch all around as you cut the shape. Turn the allowance under and baste it about halfway between the folded edge and the cut edge. It is now ready to lay wrong side down on the base fabric and blind stitch into place.

Second method (sometimes called Hawaiian): Leave an allowance of only ⅛ inch beyond the traced line. After cutting out the decorative piece lay it on the base piece and pin it in place. Then baste around the outline, about ⅜ inch from the raw edge. Tuck the allowance under with the tips of your fingers and with the point of the needle as you blindstitch. The most complex

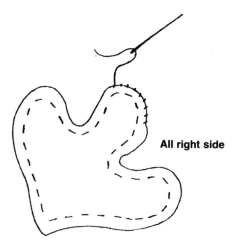

All right side

curves and scallops and sawtooth edges can be handled in this way, with only an occasional clip at the sharp inward curves and Vs.

There are a few problem areas in appliqué and a few good tricks for overcoming them. Sharp points—the ends of flower petals or leaves—should be folded three times. The first fold is straight across so that the sharp point is squared off completely. Then fold one edge under, then the other, to reform a point. There may be excess fabric in these last two folds, making extra bulk or showing out from under the edge. Clip off as much as is necessary without endangering the smooth edge or

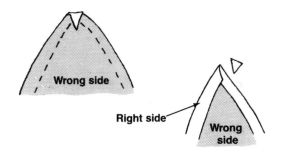

Wrong side

Right side

Wrong side

causing it to ravel. The point should now be sharp, smooth, and ready to blindstitch.

Small circles, such as little round grapes or currants, sometimes cause consternation to first-time appliqué artists. The trick is somewhat like making a Yo-Yo. Cut the circle almost twice the finished diameter—⅞ inch for a ½-inch grape. Run a line of fine gathering stitches close to the edge. Pull the gathers until the raw edges do not quite meet in the center—no real bump should form. Fasten off the gathering thread and distribute the fullness as evenly and smoothly as possible. Shape the smooth circle with your fingers and blindstitch it in place. The gathered edges will fill the grape or currant and give it a lifelike raised look, almost as though it had been stuffed.

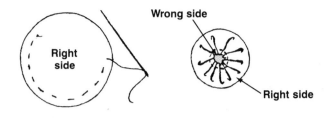

Sharp inward curves are not only hard to turn but difficult to keep in place, smooth and unraveled. For designs with many of these deep indentations, the Hawaiian method is better. With either method it may be necessary to make tiny clips around the curves to release the fabric in the allowance and let it turn under easily. It may also be necessary to take a few extra stitches closer together in this area.

The beautiful trailing vines found in so many nineteenth-century appliqué quilts are made of yards of fine bias-cut strips, not everyone's favorite fabric technique! The first step to bias perfection is perfect bias, cut at a true 45° to the straight grain of the fabric. If in doubt about the cutting and piecing of bias, you will find entire chapters on it in any basic sewing book. The simplest way to find the true bias in fabric is to fold a piece so that the cross grain is lying directly on the length grain—the resulting fold is then an exact bias.

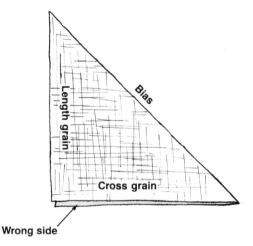

Once you've found the bias and cut strips, then comes the question of handling them so that the edges are smooth and the width consistent.

The strips should be cut no more than twice the desired finished width, but wide enough to allow turned edges of ⅛ to ¼ inch. (There will be more later about bias finished to ¼ inch or less.) For a ½-inch finished strip, cut a bias fabric strip no more than 1 inch wide. Cut a firm paper strip a scant ½ inch wide. Lay the paper strip on the wrong side of the fabric strip,

fold the edges over the paper and press gently with a steam iron. Move the paper along the strip and repeat. It is possible to prepare yards of bias vine in this way. It will now twist and turn gracefully without changing width, provided you do not stretch it at any point. Lay it down gently on the background and pin it in place. Blindstitch it, again without stretching or pulling to distort it.

Extremely narrow bias, down to a scant ⅛ inch finished, can be made by another special technique. Cut the bias strips slightly less than four times the desired finished width. Fold the strip with wrong sides together along the center and press very gently. The raw edges should meet exactly. Lay the folded piece on the base fabric, following the desired pattern, being sure not to stretch or distort it. Using a fine running stitch, seam the bias to the base fabric, always working slightly closer to the raw edges than to the folded edge. Press the folded edge over to cover the raw edges and blindstitch it in

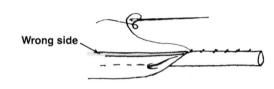

place. The effect will be slightly padded or corded, very even, and finer in width than is possible in any other way.

The all-important stitch for appliqué is called a blindstitch, not because anyone should go blind doing it, but because it should be invisible. The method is easy; perfecting it takes a little longer. Hide the knot of the thread under the edge of the decorative fabric piece. Pull the needle out exactly in the folded edge, then put it through the base fabric as close to this point as is possible. Carry the stitch under the base fabric for less than ¼ inch (the tinier the stitch, the better, up to a point) and up through the folded edge of the decorative fabric again. Then over the edge, down, and for that

very short distance under the base fabric again. Up, over, and down—it soon becomes quite rhythmic.

Never pull the stitches so tight that deep indentations form along the edge. Practice should achieve smoothness and almost total invisibility.

QUILTING AND FINISHING

The most delightful phrases are used in connection with the finishing of quilts. Quilters speak of "the sandwich," "marking out," and "putting in." All of these phrases are quite self-explanatory. The finished quilt top, neatly seamed together and pressed, is layered with the batting and backing to make a huge fabric "sandwich," which is then stitched together with tiny quilting stitches. The areas to be quilted with designs must be "marked out" lightly on the surface for accuracy in stitching the elaborate designs, such as the Pieced Flower with Stuffed Work, p. 220. If a frame is to be used when quilting, the piece must be "put in" neatly and carefully so that all edges are straight.

When cutting all of the large pieces such as long side borders or backing pieces, trim off the selvage, which can shrink in washing and cause distortion of the quilt surface. Piece the backing together so that it is slightly—an inch or two—larger than the completed top. Cut the batting to the same size as the backing.

Lay the backing right side down on a large flat surface—the floor is the only one available to most home quilters. Smooth the batting over the backing. Lay the top wrong side down on the batting and start pinning from the center out. Pin and then baste lengthwise, crosswise, and diagonally out to the corners.

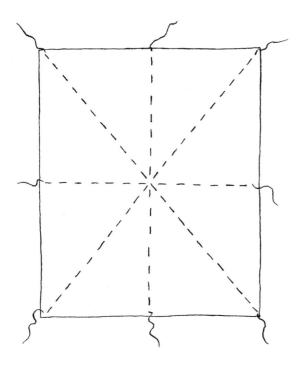

The matter of quilting with or without a frame or of using a lap frame or a standing frame must be decided by each individual on the basis of space and time. If you find it convenient to quilt in odd hours in front of the television or at a friend's house, you will find lap-quilting without a frame or with a small portable frame your best bet. If you have the space for a large frame, there is a certain professionalism and the joy of seeing the quilt in progress in the frame that are appealing. The large standing frame also accommodates more than one quilter.

Each frame has its own specifications for "putting in" the quilt. On large frames the quilt is generally attached with stitching to fabric wrapped on the rods along the sides. At its simplest, this large frame is what Ruth Finley (in *Old Patchwork Quilts and the Women Who Made Them*, 1929) calls "four stout sticks" pegged or clamped together and set up on chair backs or saw horses for use. There are smaller lap versions of this same type of frame and there are hoop frames—both standing and lap size—that work exactly like large embroidery hoops. If you want to dispense with frames altogether, you will have to baste more so that there is no slippage in the layers.

The stitch for quilting is the simplest of running stitches—the trick is in keeping it as even as possible, on both the top and bottom. The knot must be made large enough to hold, but small enough so that it will slip through the weave of the backing and hide itself in the batting. One way of making this happen is by running the needle in on a slant and giving the knot a slight tug, just enough to pull it through the backing fabric. As you start the running stitch, you may take a small backstitch to keep the knot from traveling out through the top layer. The end can be fastened with a backstitch and then the thread run for an inch or so between the layers before being cut off.

In many cases all of the quilting is worked as an outline and in multiple rows as echoes around the shapes of the pieces so that no marking is necessary. When marking is required, it should be kept as invisible as possible in the finished quilt. Many people find that a very fine hard pencil will make just enough of a mark to work by, which will virtually disappear of its own accord. Excess can often be removed with a clean art gum eraser or will wash out. There are now several pen and pencil products available which can be wiped off with a wet cloth after the quilting is completed. It is advisable to pretest these on samples of the exact fabrics and batting to be used in the quilt.

There are three standard ways of finishing a quilt edge. One way much favored by our grandmothers was done by folding the excess backing over the edge and fastening it to the front with a blind stitch so that it looked like a binding. To prepare for this be sure that you have left enough excess width and length on the backing fabric. When the quilting has been completed, trim the batting to the edge of the top. Then trim the backing so that you have an even amount all around, at least ½ inch, or more if you want a wider binding effect. The ½-inch edge will make a binding of about ¼ inch. Fold the raw edge evenly to slightly less than ¼ inch, then fold that edge over the quilt to form a narrow binding effect on the top. Pin the binding in place and blindstitch.

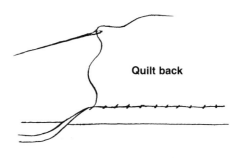

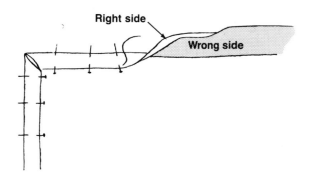

There is much discussion about the merits of straight or bias binding applied to quilts. Two tips apply to both. After the quilt has been finished and removed from the frame, measure the length and width across and along the center where the measurement is as true as possible, not along the edges where you may stretch the measurement as you go. Whether the strips are cut on the straight or the bias, they should be *true* straight and *true* bias (see the section on appliqué), and measured, marked, and cut with precision. The cut width should be slightly more than four times the finished width.

The standard way to apply binding is to lay it right side to right side along the edge of the quilt top, pinning it in place as measured, stretching neither the quilt edge nor the binding. Taking a seam of less than one quarter of the cut width, stitch the binding through all layers of the quilt. Fold it over the edge, tuck the raw edge under

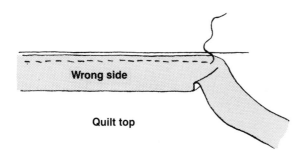

along the backing, and blindstitch. The binding may be measured and cut continuously to allow enough for a miter at each corner or cut in four pieces, two for the length and two for the width of the quilt. Wider straight bindings, like the one on the Amish Double Nine Patch, p. 217, should always be cut in four pieces.

A NOTE ABOUT THE PATTERNS

When the quilters of the past designed the remarkable pieces in this book, they were not always aware that they were creating works of art for posterity. No doubt a woman might know that a certain quilt was her "masterpiece" and the time and skill that went into it ensured a nearly perfect outcome, the most beautiful thing she'd ever made in her life. A quilt of this type was often treated with great respect by her family and neighbors, and so it has come down to us in excellent condition.

Other quilts were made of whatever was handy, but by women with an instinctive sense of color and design. Some of these are so graphic and strong and glowing that they beckon to today's quilters to repeat the performance.

Both types of quilts have been chosen for patterns in this book—some simple enough for the absolute beginner, some challenging the skilled quilter to make a new twentieth-century masterpiece. The patterns have been interpreted from the color plates with care so that all blocks, borders, and so forth are in as near proper proportion as is possible. When copying an antique quilt, only a guess can be made as to the exact size of the quilt or of the pieces in it before years of washing and folding altered the original. Therefore, the unquilted and unwashed dimensions of the quilt tops given with the patterns vary slightly from the measurements given with the pictures.

In some of the more primitive designs no two blocks are alike. Perhaps more than one person cut and stitched. Perhaps it was the first quilt made by a young girl. Perhaps the maker lived in an area where even a ruler was a luxury. The best that can be done to re-create the design is to pick the best block, copy it, and proportion the sashes, borders, and so forth so that the original charm is not lost.

In some cases true inaccuracies seem to have crept into a well-planned design. In Old Maid's Ramble, p. 234, the border is proportioned to work well, but on one side the fabric may have been stretched a little as it was seamed to the main quilt top. Again, perhaps two people worked on it and one was not as careful as the other with accurate seam allowances, and so forth. Whatever the cause, it was easy to correct when re-drawing the pattern pieces and diagrams, and so it is presented in a more symmetrical way.

The block patterns, as given, are useful in many other ways than that in which they are pictured. Every quiltmaker over the centuries has taken traditional ideas and made them her own. The colors, the settings, the size can all be changed to fit a new need and a new style. It is wise to check the block pattern by making a sample block in the fabrics chosen. It is possible to change lines infinitesimally in making a stiff paper pattern—enough to make tiny pieces like those in the Pieced Flower with Stuffed Work on p. 220 very difficult to handle. Seeing the colors actually put together is different from seeing them in your head. Last of all, fabrics and grain lines should be experienced, not just thought out on paper.

With care and proper planning the patterns in this book should enable twentieth-century quilters to repeat the wonderful achievements of their forebears. Starting with such simple beauties as Pieced Triangles, p. 267, and the Rose Spray, p. 256, any dedicated quilter should be able to move on to Feathered World Without End, p. 247, and Stars, Leaves, and Currants, p. 225.

LIST OF SOURCES

Suggested mail-order sources for quilting supplies, templates, books, and patterns:

Quilts & Other Comforts
Box 394
Wheatridge, Colorado   80033

Cabin Fever Calicoes
Box 6256
Washington, D.C.   20015

Ginger Snap Station
P.O. Box 81086
Atlanta, Georgia   30341

Mrs. Wigg's Cabbage Patch, Inc.
2600 Beaver Avenue
Des Moines, Iowa   50310

The Silver Thimble
249 High Street
Ipswich, Massachusetts   01938

The Quiltworks
218 3rd Avenue
Minneapolis, Minnesota   55401

Quilt Country
500 Nichols Road
Kansas City, Missouri   64112

Mail-in
P.O. Box 157
Schroon Lake, New York   12870

Gutcheon Patchworks
611 Broadway
New York, New York   10012

Cross Patch
Rt. #9
Garrison, New York   10524

Creative Quilt Center
Stearns & Foster
Box 15380
Cincinnati, Ohio 45215

Contemporary Quilts
3466 Summer Avenue
Memphis, Tennessee   38122

Great Expectations
155 Town and Country Village
Houston, Texas   77024

Let's Quilt and Sew-on
P.O. Box 29526
San Antonio, Texas   78229

Calico Country Store
10822 124th Street
Edmonton, Alberta
Canada   T5M 0H3

Suggested books for beginners:

The Perfect Patchwork Primer
by Beth Gutcheon
David McKay Company, Inc.
750 3rd Avenue
New York, New York   10017

Quick and Easy Quilting
by Bonnie Leman
Moon Over the Mountain Publishing
   Company
6700 West 44th Avenue
Wheatridge, Colorado   80033

You Can Be a Super Quilter
by Carla Hassel
Wallace-Homestead Book Company
1912 Grand Avenue
Des Moines, Iowa   50305

MARINER'S COMPASS WITH APPLIQUÉ

Diagram of quilt illustrated in plate 148

Dimensions: 95 x 81 inches.

Materials: all 45-inch fabrics.

3 yards white (if the blocks are pieced—*see note below*)

5⅝ yards white (if the blocks are appliquéd—*see note below*)

3½ yards red—includes binding

2½ yards green

5½ yards backing

Cut: Add ¼-inch seam allowance all around each piece and to each measurement given.

For each block: (Total of 30 blocks, 14 x 14 inches)
4 white #1
4 red #1, reversed
4 white #2
4 red #2, reversed
8 white #3
8 red #3, reversed
16 green #4
4 white #5 (if the blocks are pieced—*see note below*)
1 white square, 14 x 14 inches (if the blocks are

appliquéd—*see note below*)
4 red #6
4 green #7

For borders:
2 white strips, sides, 5½ x 95 inches
2 white strips, ends, 5½ x 70 inches
34 red leaves
34 green leaves

Directions: Piece the Compass medallion as shown in the diagram.

Appliqué the flowers in the block corners, as shown. Join the blocks together edge-to-edge. Seam the two side borders in place, then the two end borders. Appliqué the leaves in place, alternating colors and allowing them to come up to or over the edges of the blocks.

Use outline quilting around the Compass pieces and the flowers. Fill the white areas with crosshatch quilting. Add several rows of echo quilting around the leaves in the border. The binding should be about ¼ inch finished.

Note: Continue to piece the block, using the #5 pieces, or appliqué the medallion onto the solid white block.

Full-size pattern pieces
Add seam allowance

1

2

3

4

5

6

7

198

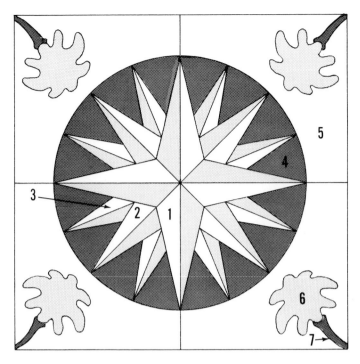

Scaled piecing and placement diagram

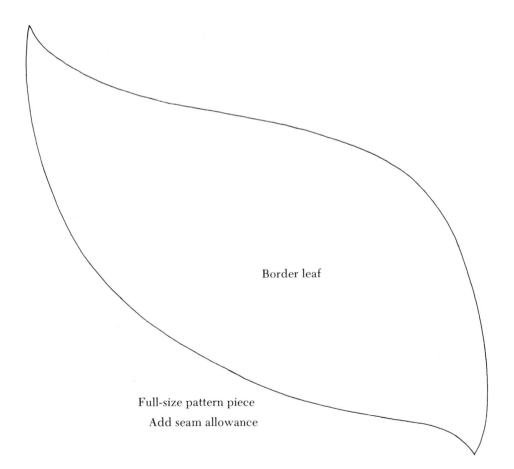

Border leaf

Full-size pattern piece
Add seam allowance

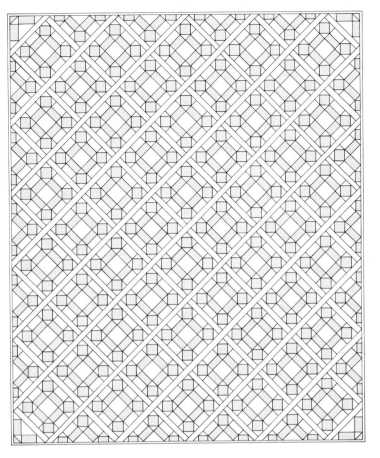

Diagram of quilt illustrated in plate 17

JOHNNY 'ROUND THE CORNER

Dimensions: 88½ x 74 inches.

Materials: all 45-inch fabrics.

6 yards blue stripe—includes sashes, backing, and binding
¾ yard white
5 yards (approximately) scraps in six to ten colors

Cut: Add ¼-inch seam allowance all around each piece and to each measurement given.

For each block: (Total of 50 blocks, 9 x 9 inches)
1 white #1
4 dark #2
4 medium #2
4 dark #3
16 medium #4

For each side triangle: (Total of 18 triangles, 9 inches on the right-angle sides—*see note below*)
1 white #5
2 dark #2

2 medium #2
1 dark #3
2 dark #6
6 medium #4
4 medium #7

For each corner triangle: (Total of 4 triangles, 6 inches on the right-angle sides)
1 white #5
2 dark #2
3 medium #4
1 dark #4

For sashes:
2 blue strips for each block, 1 x 9 inches
Long blue strips, 1 inch wide, to join all rows of blocks

Directions: The block is a true Nine Patch so it may be assembled in nine squares, then in three rows of three squares each, and so forth, according to the diagram. If the blocks are to be signed, and/or embroidered, this should be done before they are joined together.

Seam the short sashes onto two opposite sides of each block, seam the blocks into rows of one, three, five blocks, and so forth, finishing each end with side triangles, as shown.

When the edges are evenly trimmed, bind around them with very narrow binding cut from the blue sash fabric. Outline quilting may be used around each piece. If no signatures were used in the center blocks, a small quilted design might be used there.

Note: The side and corner triangles have been drafted accurately so that the quilt will go together without distortion of the fabric. After the quilt is assembled, you will find it necessary to trim about ¼ inch off each side triangle to make it absolutely even with the corners (see scaled diagram).

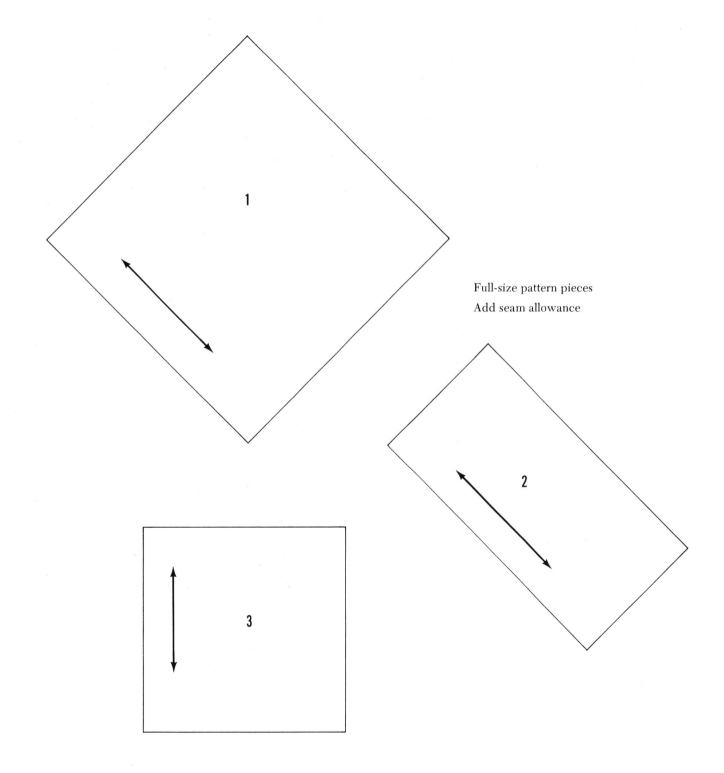

Full-size pattern pieces
Add seam allowance

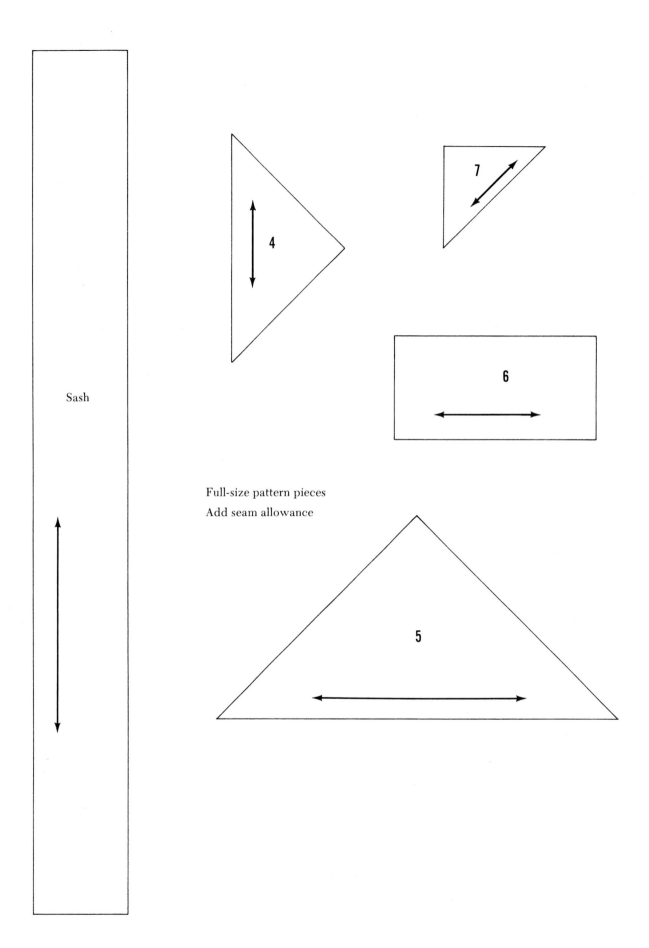

Sash

4

7

6

Full-size pattern pieces
Add seam allowance

5

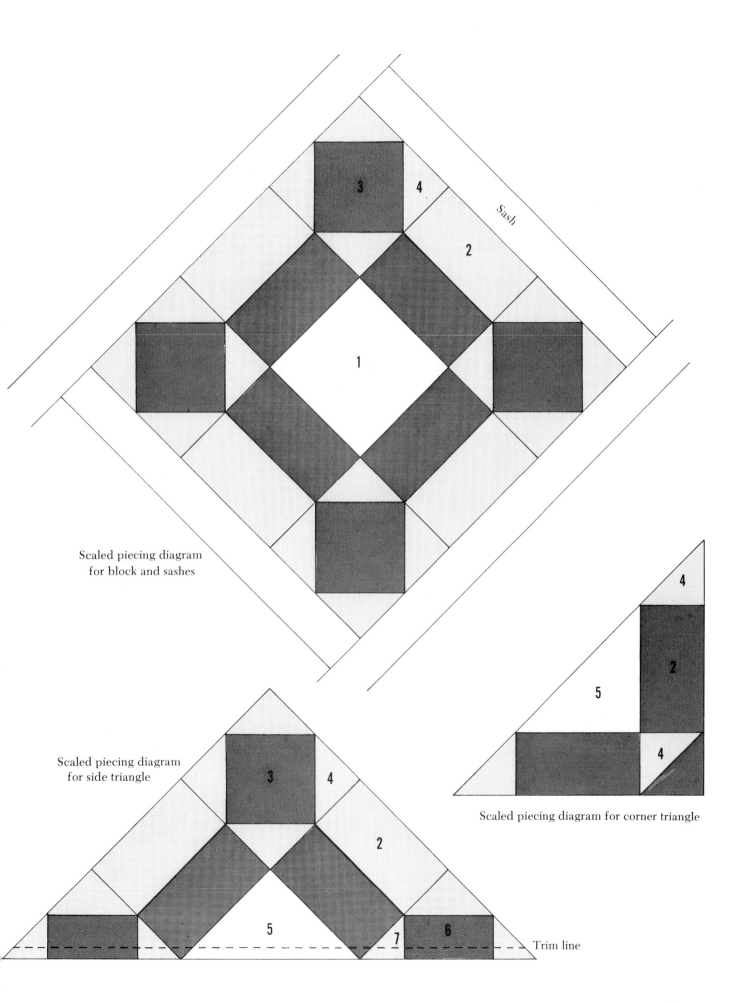

Sash

1

3   4

2

Scaled piecing diagram
for block and sashes

Scaled piecing diagram
for side triangle

3   4

2

5

7   6

Trim line

4

2

5

4

Scaled piecing diagram for corner triangle

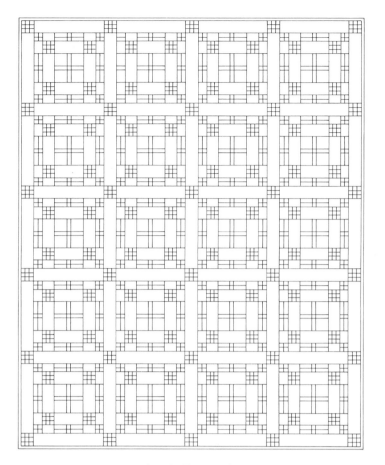

Diagram of quilt illustrated in plate 153

ROAD
TO CALIFORNIA

Dimensions: 90⅛ x 72⅝ inches.

Materials: all 45-inch fabrics.

  8 yards white—includes backing and binding.
  3 yards (approximately) scraps in dark and medium
  earth tones and some red

*Cut: Add ¼-inch seam allowance all around each piece
  and to each measurement given.*

For each block: (Total of 20 blocks, 14⅞ x 14⅞ inches)
  4 white #1
  4 dark #2
  8 white #3
  12 dark #3
  33 white #4
  28 dark #4
  8 medium #5

For each corner block: (Total of 30 blocks, 2⅝ x 2⅝
  inches)
  5 white #4
  4 red #4

For sashes:
  49 white rectangles, 2⅝ x 14⅞ inches

Directions: Piece the small checkerboard pieces first,
then make up nine units—not quite a true Nine
Patch—and assemble in three strips, then a whole
block, as illustrated. Lay all of the blocks out on a large
flat surface to determine the most pleasing color
arrangement.

Assemble the blocks in strips of five, starting and
ending with a white sash. Make up the five long sashes,
using five white pieces and six corner blocks each. Join
all of the long strips as shown in the diagram.

Quilt the outlines of the pieced blocks. Choose small
decorative quilting designs for sashes and white center
pieces. Bind the edge narrowly with white.

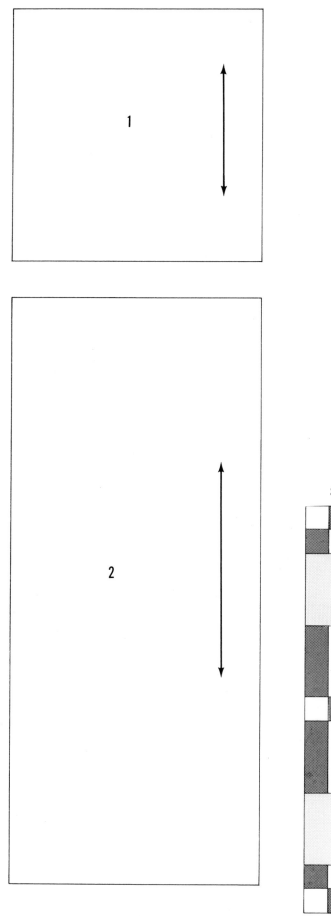

1

2

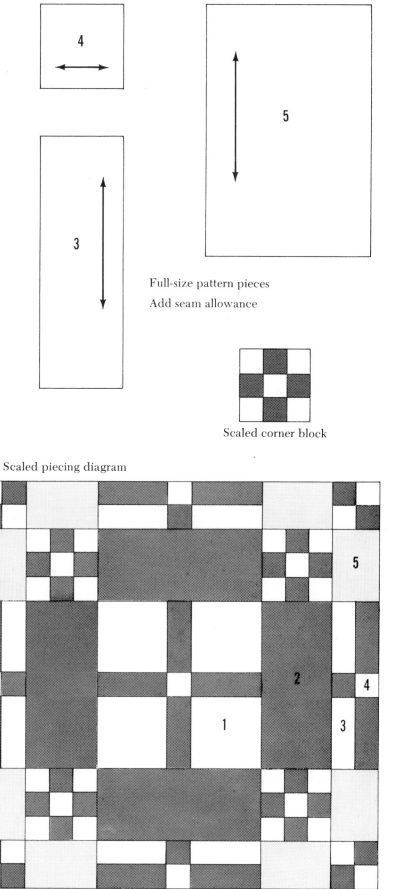

4

3

5

Full-size pattern pieces

Add seam allowance

Scaled corner block

Scaled piecing diagram

5

2

4

1

3

205

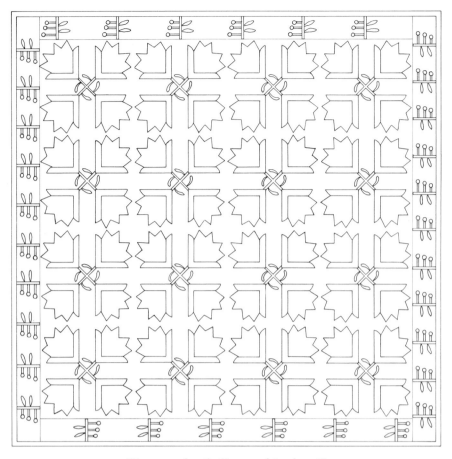

Diagram of quilt illustrated in plate 48

BLOSSOMS AND BERRIES

Dimensions: 76 x 76 inches.

Materials: all 45-inch fabrics.

  4⅞ yards white
    6 yards gray-green—includes backing
  2½ yards gold—includes binding
  1½ yards red

Cut: Add ¼-inch seam allowance all around each piece and to each measurement given.

For each block: (Total of 8 red, 8 gold, 16 x 16 inches)
  1 white square, 16 x 16 inches
  4 red or gold #1
  4 green #2
  4 green #2, reversed
  4 green #3
  12 inches green bias, ¼-inch wide

For borders:
  2 white strips, ends, 6 x 64 inches
  2 white strips, sides, 6 x 76 inches
  34 berry clusters, each:
    1 red #4
    1 gold #4
    1 green #4
    2 green #5
    11 inches green bias, ¼-inch wide

Directions: Appliqué the flowers in position, as shown on the placement diagram. Appliqué six berry clusters on each end border, ten or eleven on each side border.

Set the blocks together so that the colors alternate, two of each color in each of four rows. Add the end borders to the center piece, then the side borders.

Work outline quilting around all of the designs. Quilt in the white areas with a diagonal crosshatch or any pleasing small designs. Bind the edges in gold so that about ½ inch shows all around.

Full-size pattern pieces
Add seam allowance

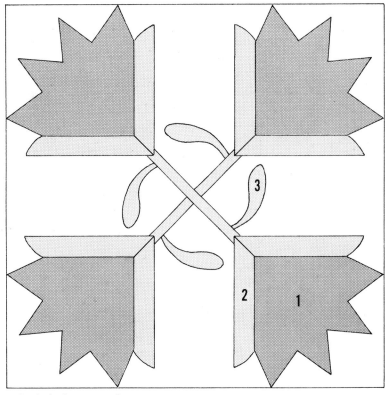

Scaled placement diagram

Scaled placement diagram
for border section

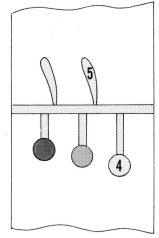

PINEAPPLE

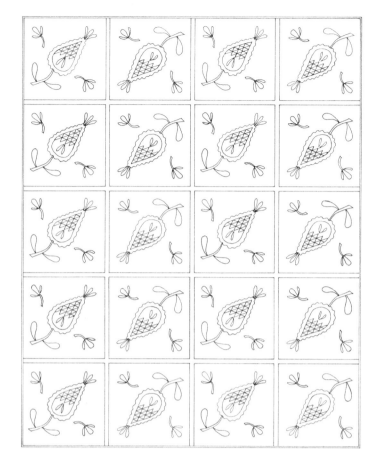

Diagram of quilt illustrated in plate 182

Dimensions: 89 x 71 inches.

Materials: all 45-inch fabrics.

5¼ yards white
6 yards green pin-dot—includes backing
3 yards orange—includes binding

Cut: Add ½-inch seam allowance all around each piece and to each measurement given.

For each block: (Total of 20 blocks, 17 x 17 inches)
1 white square, 17 x 17 inches
1 orange #1
14 orange #2
10 green #2
1 green #3
1 green #4
1 green #4, reversed
1 green #5
1 green #6
1 green #6, reversed
1 orange #7
1 orange #7, reversed

2 green #8
2 green #8, reversed
1 green #9
1 green #9, reversed
1 green #10
1 green #10, reversed
1 green #11

For sashes:
16 orange strips, 1 x 17 inches
3 orange strips, 1 x 89 inches

Directions: Piece the orange and the green #2 pieces together and attach to the orange #1 piece. Appliqué the #3 piece in place around this pieced section, and the #4 pieces on the #1 piece. Appliqué all the other pieces in place as shown on the placement diagram.

Set the Pineapple blocks together in four strips of five each with the orange sashes between. Set the rows together, alternating the direction of the Pineapples, as shown, with the long orange sashes between.

Work outline quilting around the designs and diagonal crosshatch quilting in the white areas. Bind the edges with very narrow, orange bias binding.

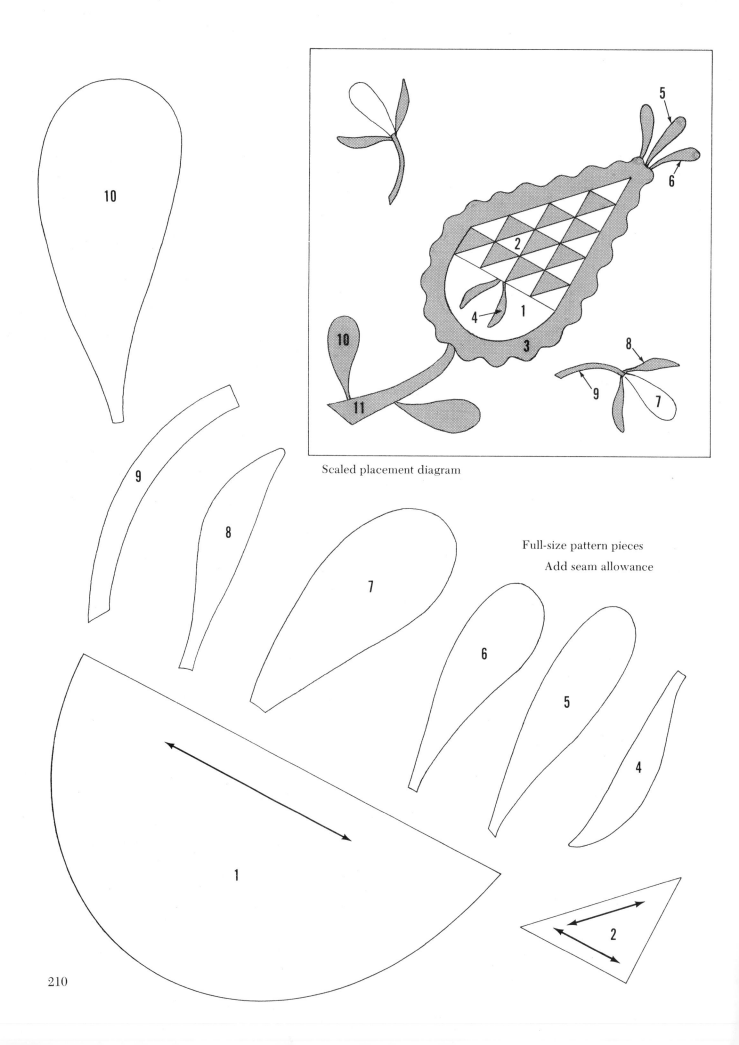

Scaled placement diagram

Full-size pattern pieces

Add seam allowance

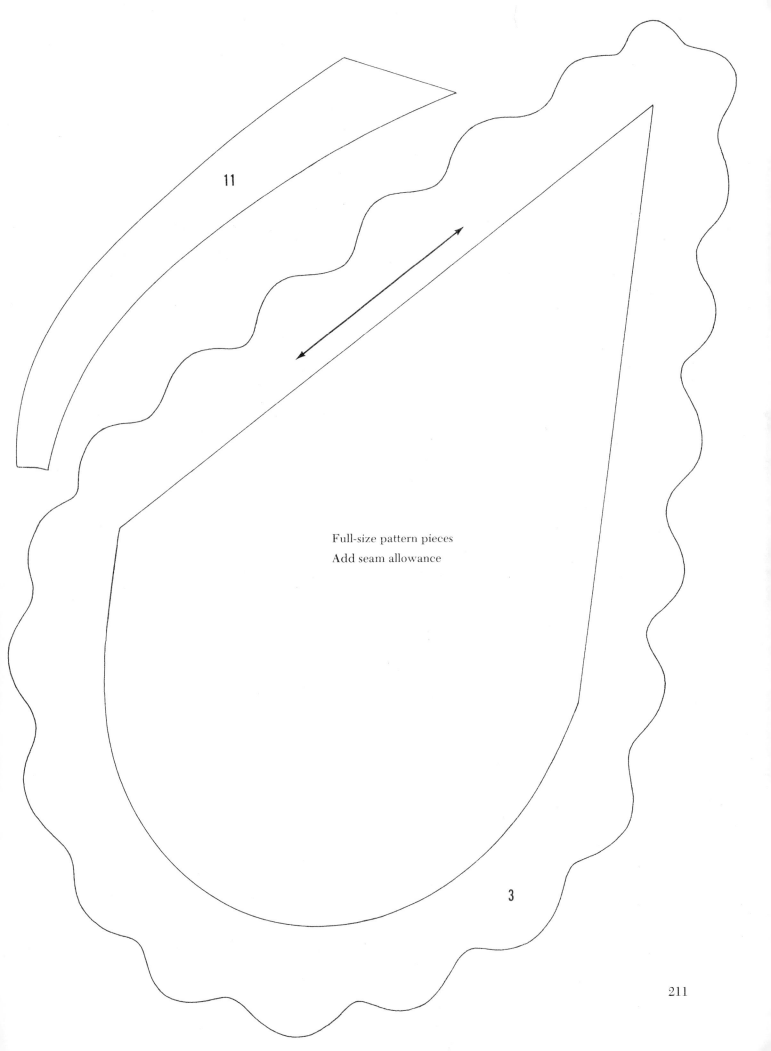

11

Full-size pattern pieces
Add seam allowance

3

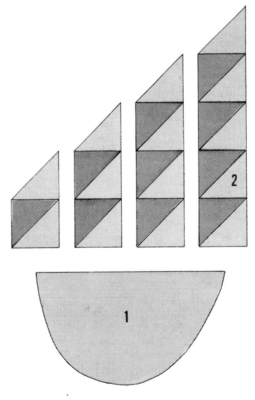

Scaled piecing diagram for center

FLOWERING FERN

Diagram of quilt illustrated in plate 19

Dimensions: 96 x 96 inches.

Materials: all 45-inch fabrics.

6½ yards white
8 yards green—includes backing and binding
½ yard gold
1 yard dark red

Cut: Add ¼-inch seam allowance all around each piece and to each measurement given.

For each block: (Total of 4 blocks, 34 x 34 inches)
1 white square, 34 x 34 inches
8 gold #1
4 green #2
4 green complete #3 (*see note below*)
8 gold #4
8 red #5
8 green #6
8 green #6, reversed
4 green #7
4 green #8

For borders:
2 white strips, sides, 14 x 96 inches
2 white strips, ends, 14 x 68 inches
14 green complete #3 (cut off—*see note below*)
10 gold #4
10 red #5
10 green #6
10 green #6, reversed
10 green #8 (cut off)

Directions: Piece the center Star as shown in the diagram, with green #2 pieces set into four sides. Appliqué this piece and all leaf and flower pieces to white background block, as shown. Appliqué three large leaves and two flowers on each end border, four leaves and three flowers on each side border.

Seam together the four center blocks, then add the end borders and last the side borders. Quilt along the lines marked on the large leaves and around each part of the appliquéd pieces. Cover the entire background with diagonal crosshatch quilting. Finish the end with a binding made by bringing the back over the edges of the front (see pp. 193–194).

Note: Piece pattern #3a to #3b—cut either on fold of fabric or with straight seam down center line of #3b.

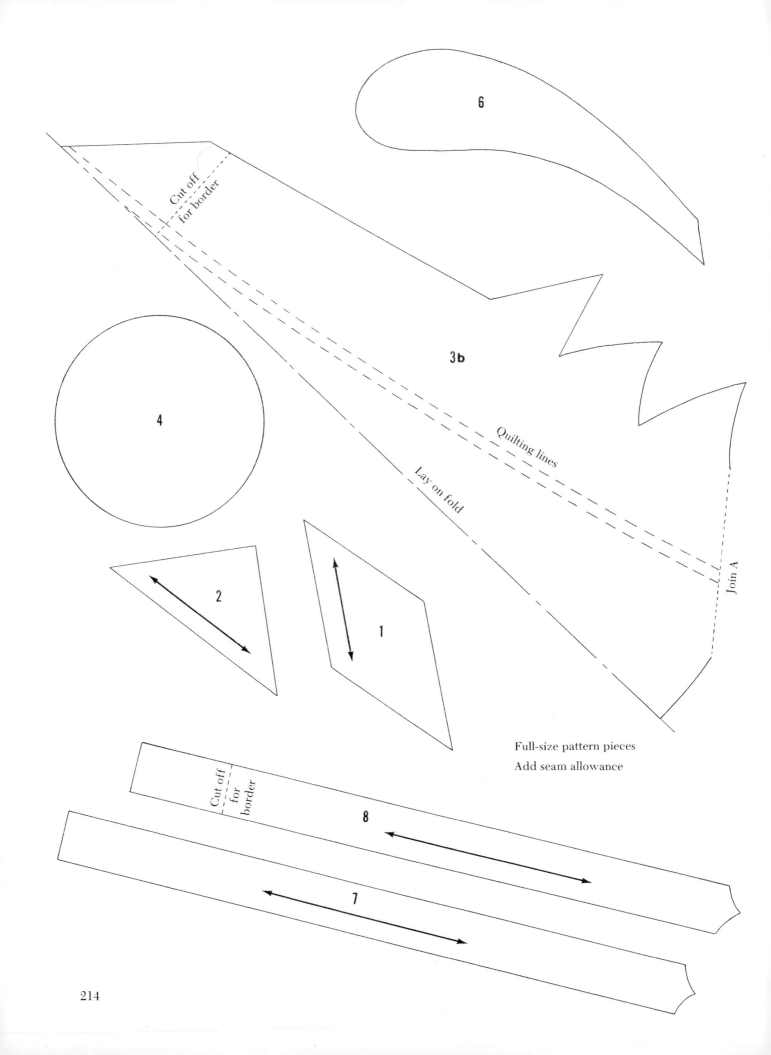

6

Cut off for border

3b

4

Quilting lines

Lay on fold

Join A

2

1

Full-size pattern pieces

Add seam allowance

Cut off for border

8

7

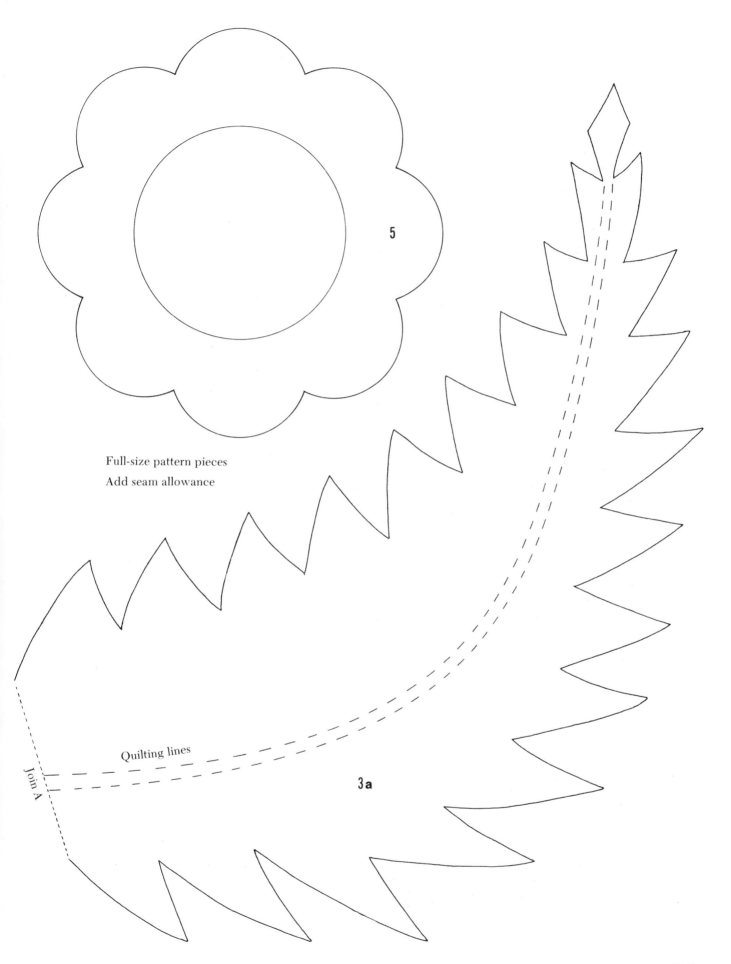

5

Full-size pattern pieces
Add seam allowance

Quilting lines

Join A

3a

Scaled piecing and placement diagram

AMISH DOUBLE NINE PATCH

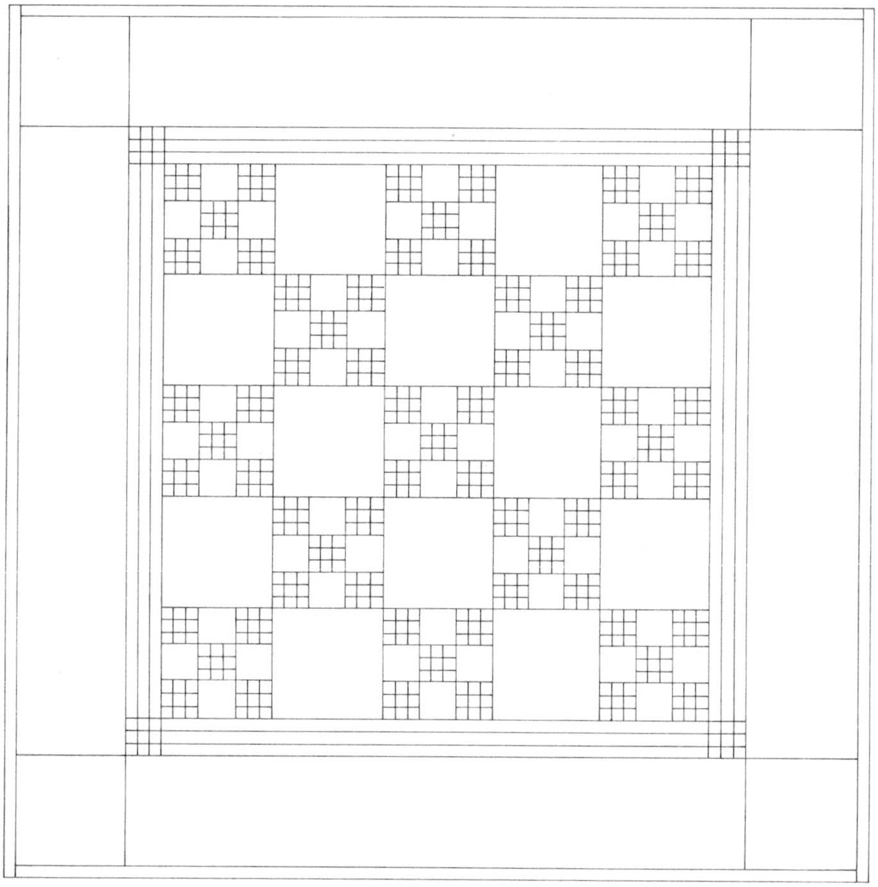

Diagram of quilt illustrated in plate 40

Dimensions: 79⅞ x 79⅞ inches.

Materials: all 45-inch fabrics (if cotton is used).

2⅞ yards dark green
¾ yard red
½ yard bright blue
2¼ yards purple—includes narrow border or binding
1½ yards pink
4⅝ yards any backing
Scraps of navy and other colors

Materials: all 54- or 60-inch fabrics (if wool is used).
2¼ yards dark green
½ yard red
2¼ yards purple—includes narrow border or binding
⅝ yard pink (cut crosswise)
4⅝ yards bright blue—includes backing
Scraps of navy and other colors

Cut: Add ¼-inch seam allowance all around each piece and to each measurement given.

For each Double Nine Patch block: (Total of 13 blocks, 10⅛ x 10⅛ inches)
4 red #1
25 dark #2
20 dark #2

For alternating blocks:
12 dark green squares, 10⅛ inches x 10⅛ inches

For inner borders:
8 purple strips, 50⅝ x 1⅛ inches
4 pink strips, 50⅝ x 1⅛ inches
20 dark green #2
16 pink #2

For outer borders:
4 dark green rectangles, 57⅜ x 10⅛ inches
4 bright blue squares, 10⅛ inches

For narrow border or binding:
2 purple strips, ends, 2¼ x 77⅝ inches (straight grain)
2 purple strips, sides, 2¼ x 79⅞ inches (straight grain)

Directions: Piece the small Nine Patch pieces, join them with the red #1 pieces to make the Double Nine Patch blocks. Using these alternately with the dark green squares, make up the centers. Make up the Nine Patch corner blocks and the triple strips for the inner border. Add the inner and outer borders to the center piece.

Quilt the entire piece, using Wreath designs in the large squares and other suitable designs in the other areas. When trimming the edges, allow the backing and batting to remain about ¾ inch beyond the edge of the quilt top. Seam and finish the narrow border strips, top and bottom first and then sides, as is described for binding, p. 194. The finished width should be about 1¼ inches.

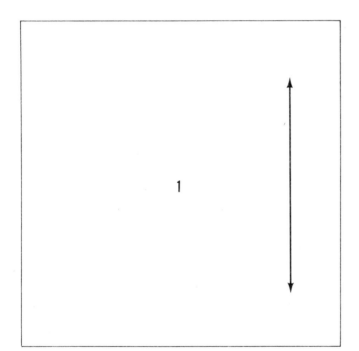

Full-size pattern pieces
Add seam allowance

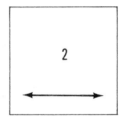

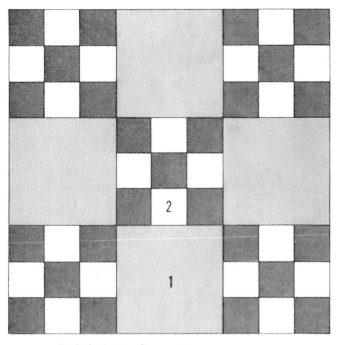

Scaled piecing diagram

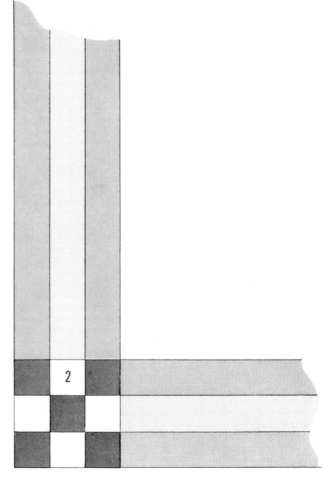

Scaled inner-border diagram

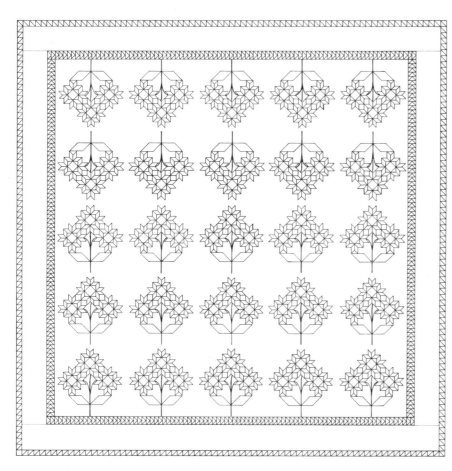

Diagram of quilt illustrated in plate 10

PIECED FLOWER
WITH
STUFFED WORK

Dimensions: 90 x 90 inches.

Materials: all 45-inch fabrics.

12 yards white—includes backing and binding.
  1¼ yards green print
  1¼ yards red print

*Cut: Add ¼-inch seam allowance all around each piece
and to each measurement given.*

For each pieced block (Total of 25 blocks, 10 x 10
    inches, 14⅛ inches on diagonal)
  1 white #1
  1 white #2
  1 green #3
  1 green #3, reversed
  3 red #4
  40 white #5
  2 green #5
  24 green #6
  24 red #6
  10 white #7
  15 inches of green bias, ⅛-inch wide

To complete center:
  16 white squares, 10 x 10 inches
  16 white triangles, 10 inches on right-angle sides
    4 white triangles, 7¹/₁₆ inches on right-angle sides

For inner border (*see note below*):
  184 green #8
  184 red #8
  368 white #9

For second border:
  2 white strips, sides, 6½ x 73⅜ inches
  2 white strips, ends, 6½ x 86⅜ inches

For outer border (*see note below*):
  73 green #8
  72 red #8
  290 white #8 (*see note below*)

Directions: Piece the twenty-five blocks and inner and
outer borders as shown.

    Trace the stuffed work design very lightly on each
white block and on the second border. Pin a very thin

backing—batiste is good—on the wrong side of each block. With pastel thread work a medium size running stitch all around the design lines—the stitches should be larger than those for quilting but not as large as for basting. Cut small holes in the backing and insert pieces of batting, pushing them into all areas of the design with a knitting needle. Or, using a large tapestry needle, run 4-ply synthetic yarn back and forth through the backing until it fills the design area. Leave loops of the yarn at each side, then cut them off and work the raw ends into the space to be filled.

Piece together the entire center, alternating pieced and white blocks, and finishing the edges with the triangles. Add the side inner borders, then the end inner borders. Add the white second borders in the same order, and finally the pieced outer borders.

Quilt around all of the stuffed work, then remove the pastel stitches. Outline quilt the pieced blocks. Fill all of the areas between with closely spaced parallel lines of quilting. Finish the edge with a very narrow binding—preferably the type brought over from the back (see pp. 193–194).

Note: Because much of the center is on the bias and it is difficult to give an exact measurement diagonally across the blocks, your measurements may change slightly from the original, so you may require more or less of the tiny border pieces.

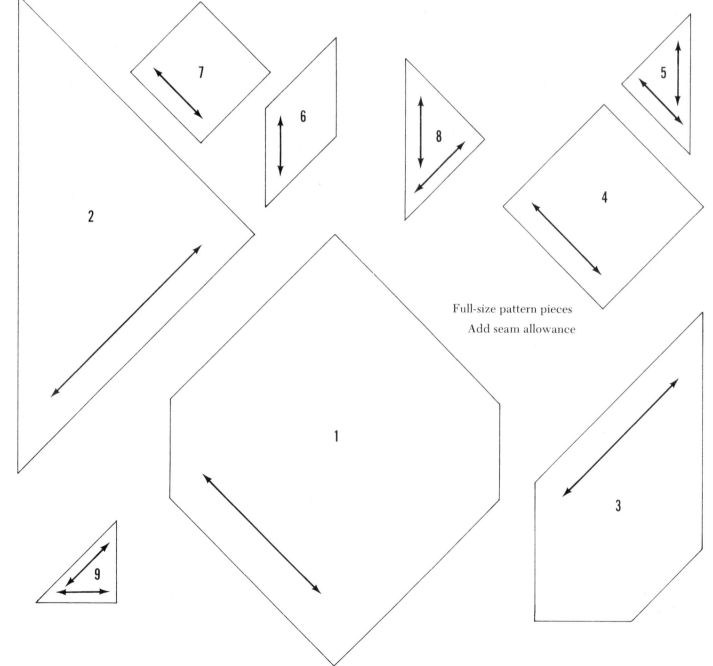

Full-size pattern pieces

Add seam allowance

Full-size white block with quilting design

222

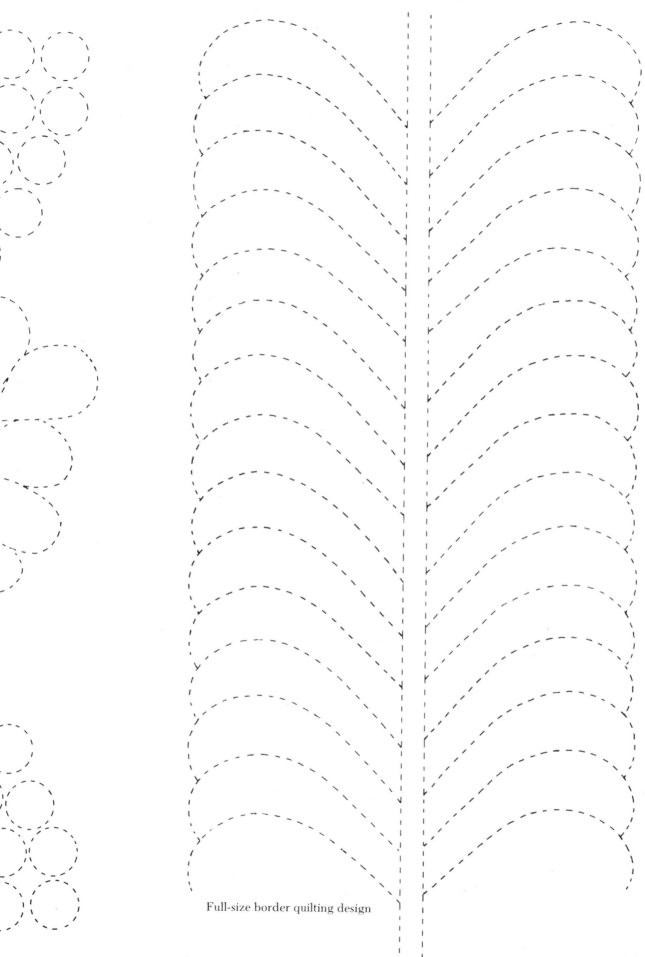

Full-size border quilting design

Scaled border diagrams

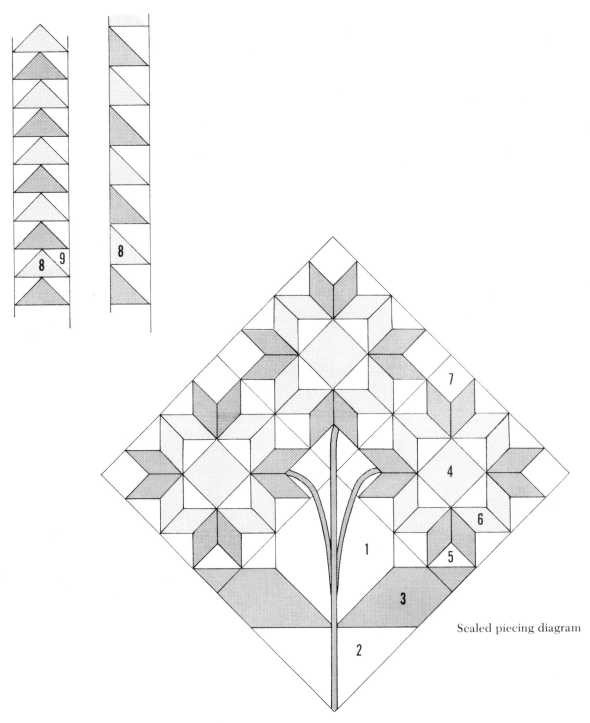

Scaled piecing diagram

STARS, LEAVES, AND CURRANTS

Diagram of quilt illustrated in plate 11

Dimensions: 84 x 84 inches.

Materials: all 45-inch fabrics.

12 yards white—includes backing and binding
2 yards red
2 yards navy

Cut: Add ¼-inch seam allowance all around each piece and to each measurement given.

For each block: (Total of 9 blocks, 22 x 22 inches)
1 white square, 22 x 22 inches
1 red #1
1 navy #2
4 navy #3
8 red #4
4 navy #5
4 navy bias #6
32 red #7
28 navy #7

For sashes:
6 white strips, 22 x 4½ inches
2 white strips, 75 x 4½ inches

For borders:
2 white strips, sides, 75 x 4½ inches
2 white strips, ends, 84 x 4½ inches

For sash and border appliqué:
12 red #1
12 navy #2
32 red #7
32 navy #7

Directions: Appliqué each block. Join the blocks into three rows with the short sashes. Join the rows with the long sashes. Add the side and end borders. Appliqué the intersecting areas to complete the design.

Quilt around all of the appliqué motifs. Quilt the designs in the blocks, sashes, and borders. Finish the edges with a narrow white binding.

225

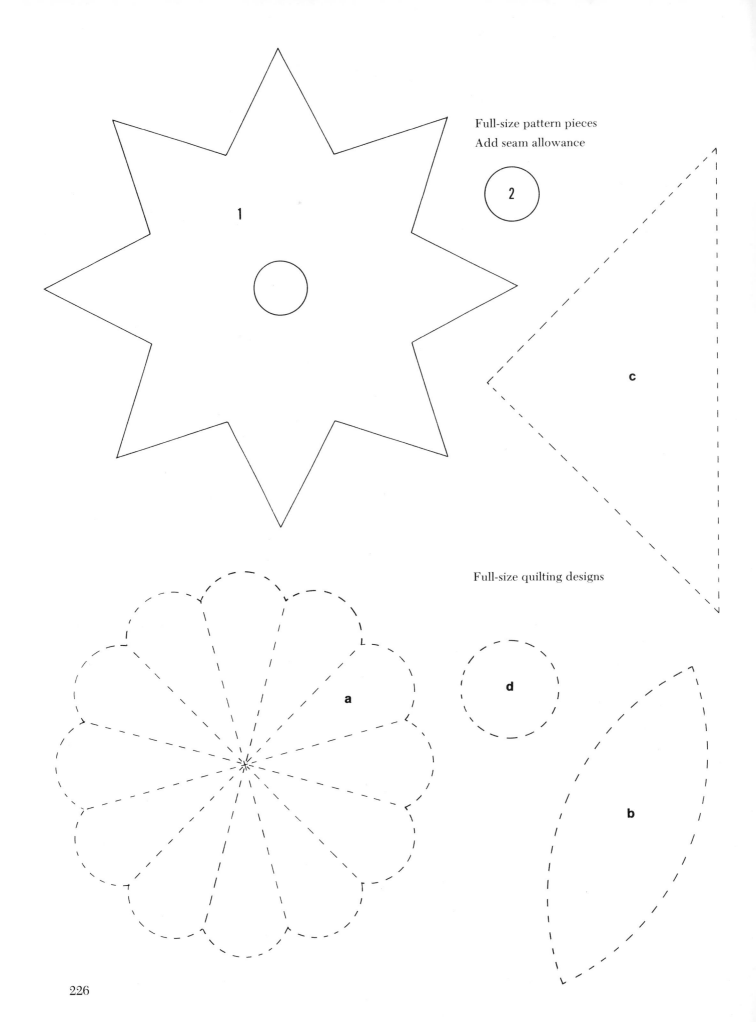

Full-size pattern pieces

Add seam allowance

2

1

c

Full-size quilting designs

a

d

b

226

Full-size pattern pieces
Add seam allowance

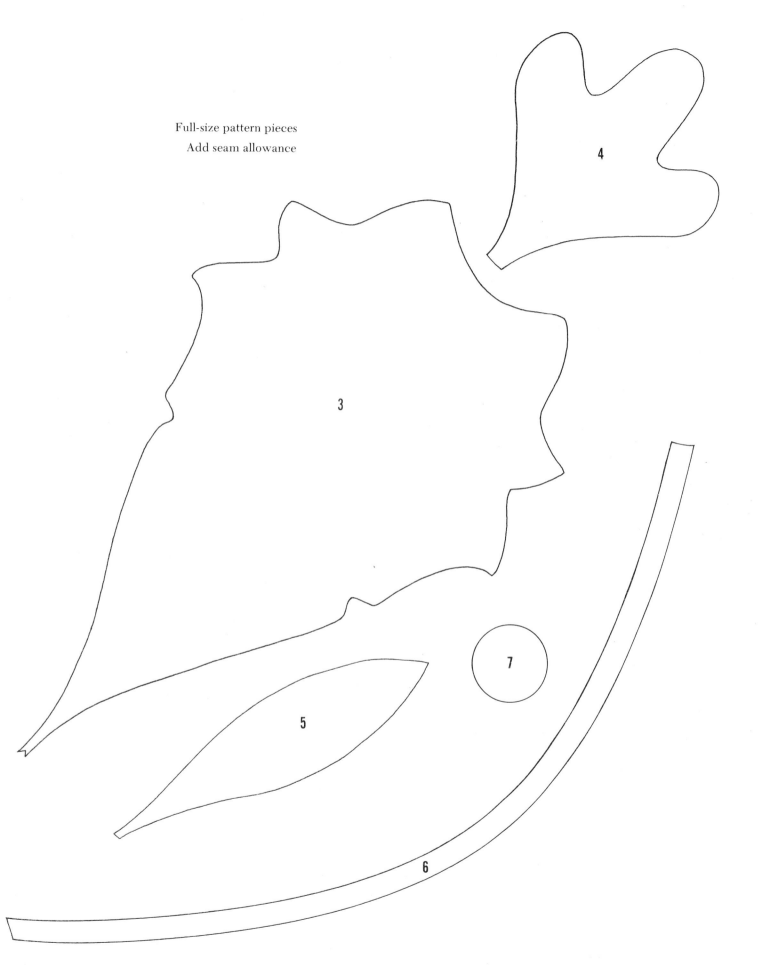

4

3

5

7

6

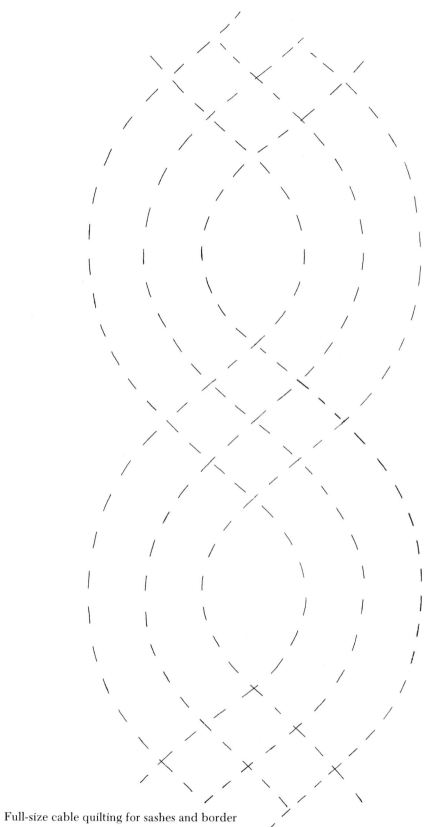

Full-size cable quilting for sashes and border

Scaled placement and quilting diagram

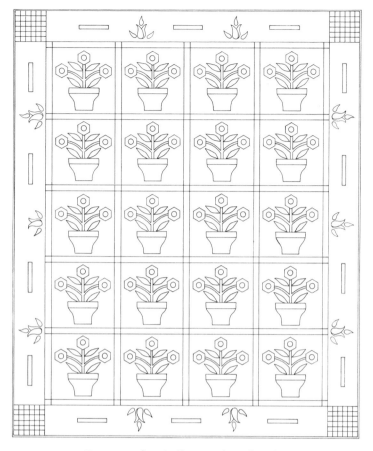

Diagram of quilt illustrated in plate 21

POT OF FLOWERS

Dimensions: 99 x 82½ inches.

Materials: all 45-inch fabrics.

8 yards white
9 yards soft green—includes backing and binding
½ yard green-and-white check
½ yard medium green
½ yard orange
½ yard (approximately) print scraps

Cut: Add ¼-inch seam allowance all around each piece and to each measurement given.

For each block: (Total of 20 blocks, 15 x 15 inches)
1 white square, 15 x 15 inches
1 green check #1
1 orange #2
3 print #3
2 medium green #4
2 medium green #4, reversed
1 medium green #5 (bias)
1 medium green #5, reversed (bias)
1 medium green #6
3 orange #7

For sashes:
49 soft green strips, 15 x 1½ inches
30 white squares, 1½ x 1½ inches

For borders:
2 white strips, ends, 67½ x 7½ inches
2 white strips, sides, 84 x 7½ inches
14 orange strips, 7½ x 1 inches
10 appliqué motifs of:
1 soft green #8
1 soft green #9
1 soft green #10
1 soft green #10, reversed
1 soft green #11

For each border corner:
18 soft green squares, 1¼ x 1¼ inches
18 white squares, 1¼ x 1¼ inches

Directions: Appliqué each block and each border. Piece the blocks together in four strips of five, joined with the sashes. Piece together the other sashes in five strips of five, joined with the small white squares. Make up the checkerboard corners. Assemble the entire top, as shown.

Use outline quilting around the sashes and appliqué designs. Use the quilting motifs inside the blocks, reversing them for the left side. Use crosshatch quilting in the wide border areas. Bind the edge narrowly with the soft green.

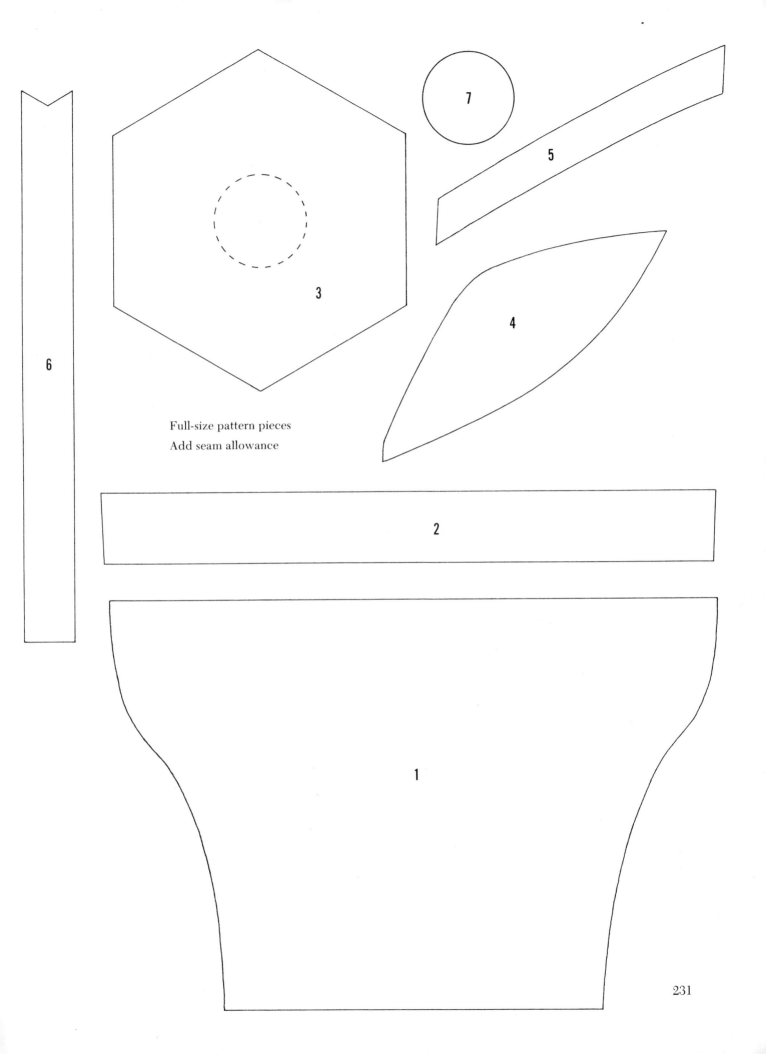

Full-size pattern pieces
Add seam allowance

231

10

b

Full-size quilting diagrams

11

9

Full-size
pattern pieces

Add seam
allowance

8

a

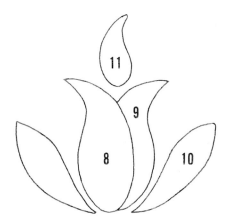

Scaled border-motif diagram

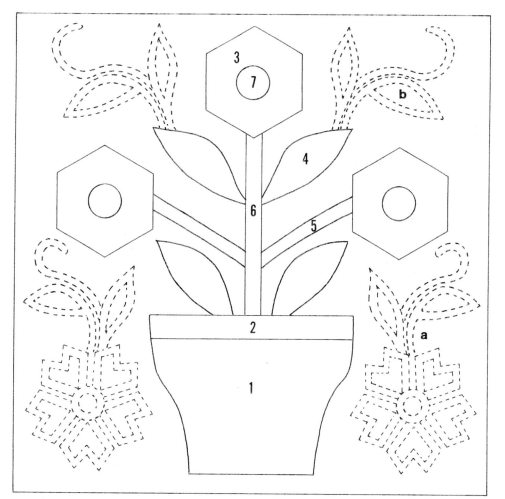

Scaled placement and quilting diagram

Diagram of quilt illustrated in plate 101

OLD MAID'S RAMBLE

Dimensions: 80 x 80 inches.

Materials: all 45-inch fabrics.

8 yards white—includes backing
4 yards red—includes binding

Cut: Add ¼-inch seam allowance all around each piece and to each measurement given.

For each block: (Total of 100 blocks, 7 x 7 inches)
2 red #1
4 white #2
6 red #3
10 white #3

For borders:
240 red triangles
240 white triangles

Directions: Piece the four squares of each block and assemble to make a complete block. Then piece four blocks together to make each unit—twenty-five units in all. Five units in each direction will form the center of the quilt.

Piece white and red triangles together alternately to make the border squares. Make a twenty-eight-square strip for each side, then two thirty-square strips for the ends, and finally a thirty-two-square strip for each side. Notice the change made for easier and more accurate piecing of the borders.

Use outline quilting all around each piece. Finish the quilt with narrow red binding.

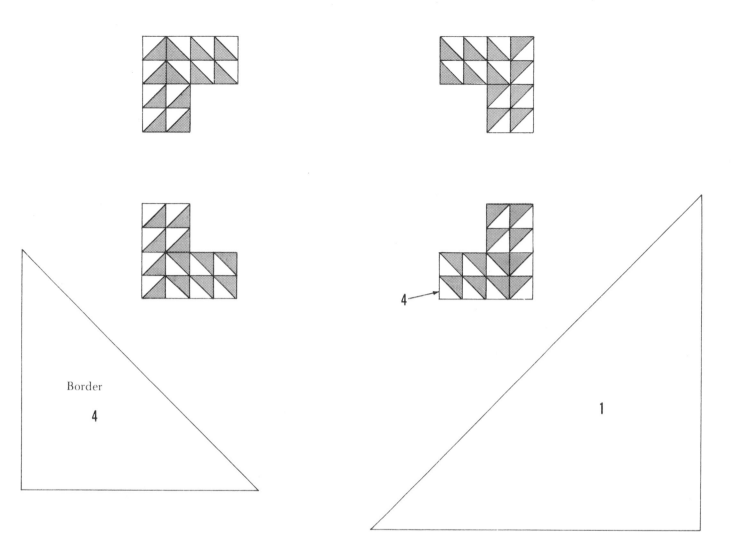

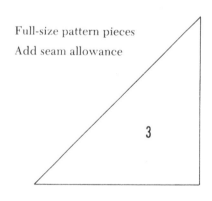

Border

4

1

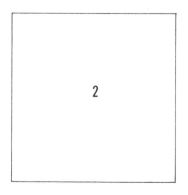

4 →

Full-size pattern pieces

Add seam allowance

3

2

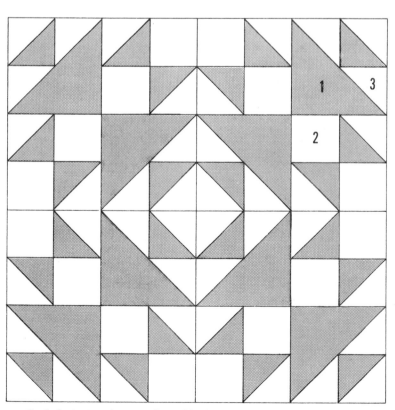

Scaled piecing diagram for 4-block unit

1

3

2

235

Diagram of quilt illustrated in plate 137

CHERRY TREES

Dimensions: 79 x 83 inches.

Materials: all 45-inch fabrics.

11 yards white—includes backing
3 yards green
4 yards red—includes binding

Cut: Add ¼-inch seam allowance all around each piece and to each measurement given.

For each main block: (Total of 13 blocks, 13 x 13 inches)
1 green #1
1 green #2
1 green #3
1 green #4 (on fold)
2 green #5
2 red #6
1 green #7
31 green #8
22 red #8

For each of 2 bottom triangles:
2 green #10
2 red #11

14 green #12
16 red #12

For each of 6 side and top triangles:
1 green #7, reversed
1 green #9
13 green #8
6 red #8

For each of 4 corner triangles:
6 green #12
3 red #12
2 green #13

For borders:
2 white strips, sides, 63 x 10 inches
2 white strips, ends, 83 x 8 inches
10 yards of green bias, ¾-inch wide
(approximate measurements)

For each of 8 bottom scallops:
2 green #15
7 red #12
14 green #12

For each of 10 side scallops:
  2 green #14
  7 red #16
  14 green #16

For each of 8 top scallops:
  1 green #17
  2½ inches of green bias, ¼-inch wide

Directions: Appliqué the motifs on each block and on the triangles and borders. Arrange the green bias in scallops on the borders, letting it lie the full ¾-inch width at the bottom of each scallop, tapering to ⅜ inch at the ends. The scallops at the bottom corners can be finished after the borders are joined.

Set the blocks together in diagonal rows, finishing the edges with the triangles. Finish small stems, and so forth, as called for, with embroidery—outline or chain stitch—using three strands of six-strand embroidery cotton.

Quilt around all appliqué designs. Quilt the remaining background with any small design—Clamshell or diagonal lines. Bind the edge with narrow red binding.

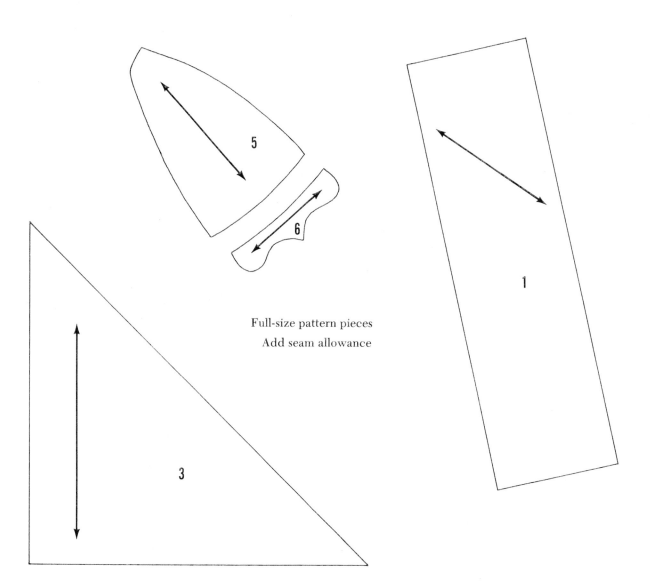

Full-size pattern pieces
Add seam allowance

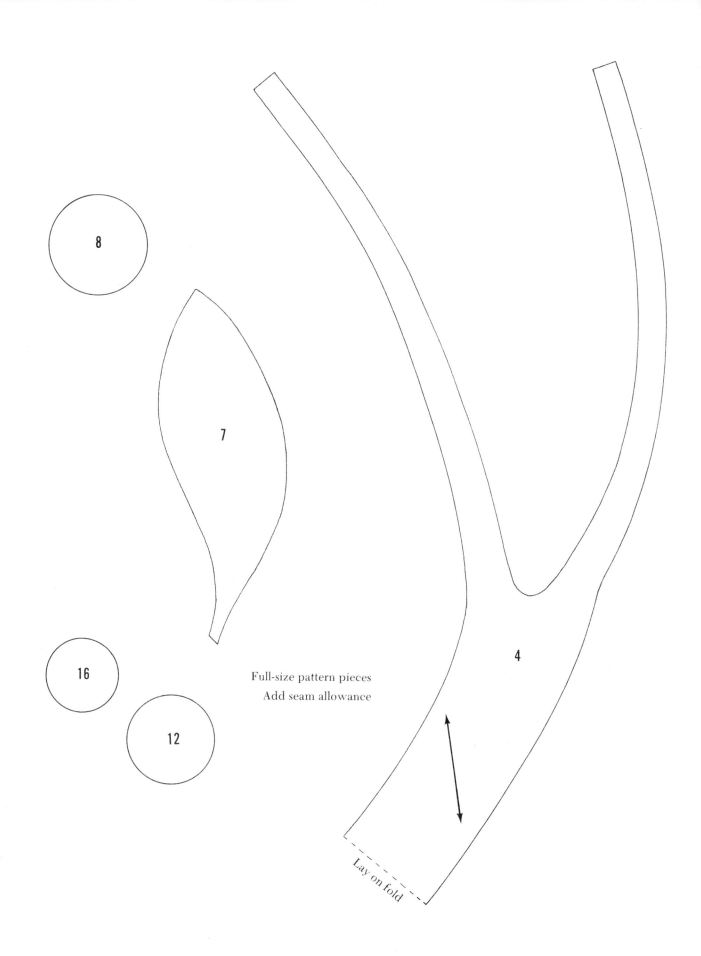

8

7

16

12

Full-size pattern pieces
Add seam allowance

4

Lay on fold

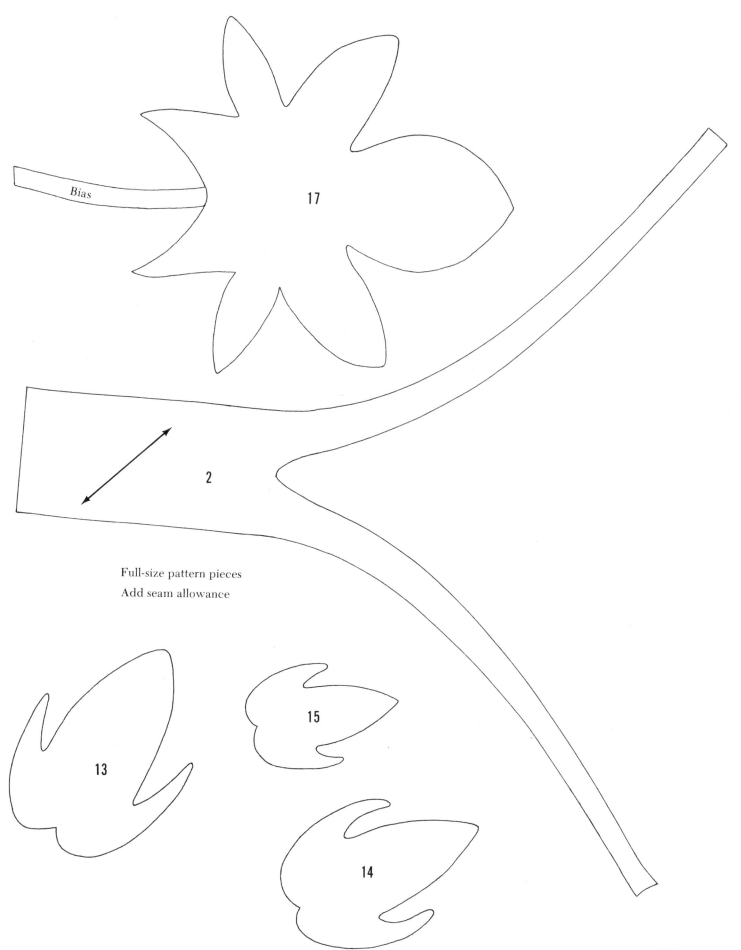

Bias

17

2

Full-size pattern pieces
Add seam allowance

13

15

14

239

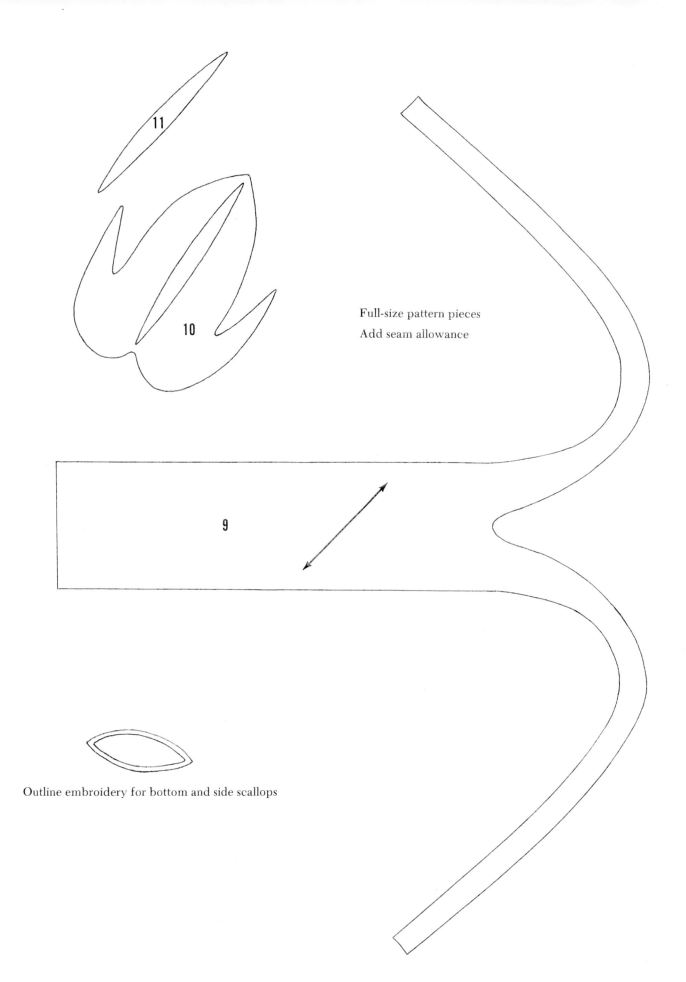

11

10

9

Full-size pattern pieces
Add seam allowance

Outline embroidery for bottom and side scallops

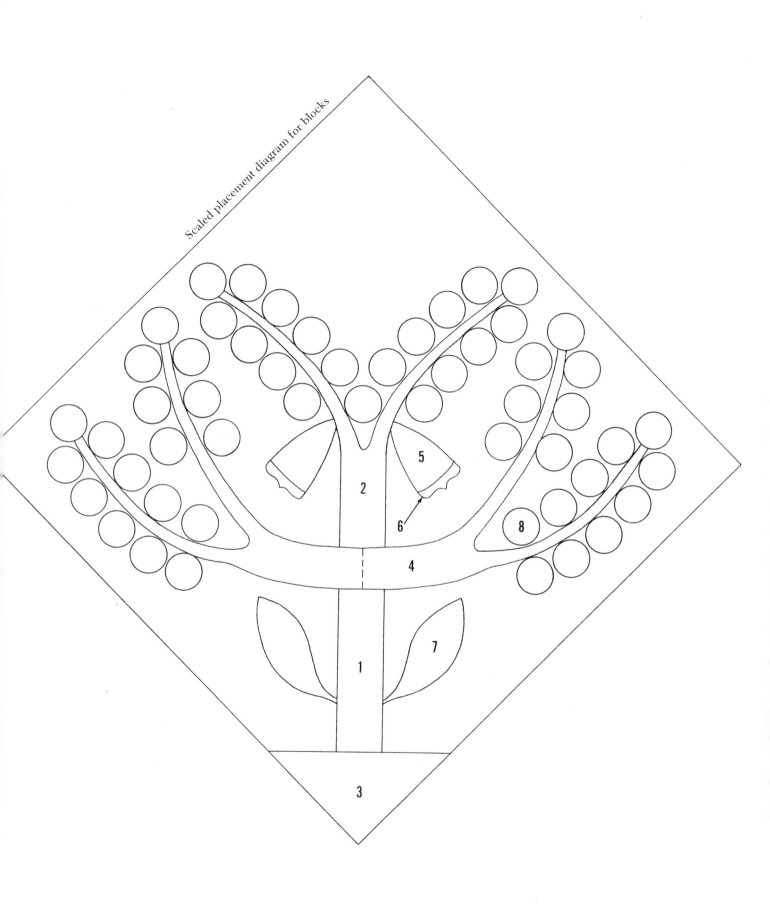

Scaled placement diagram for blocks

1
2
3
4
5
6
7
8

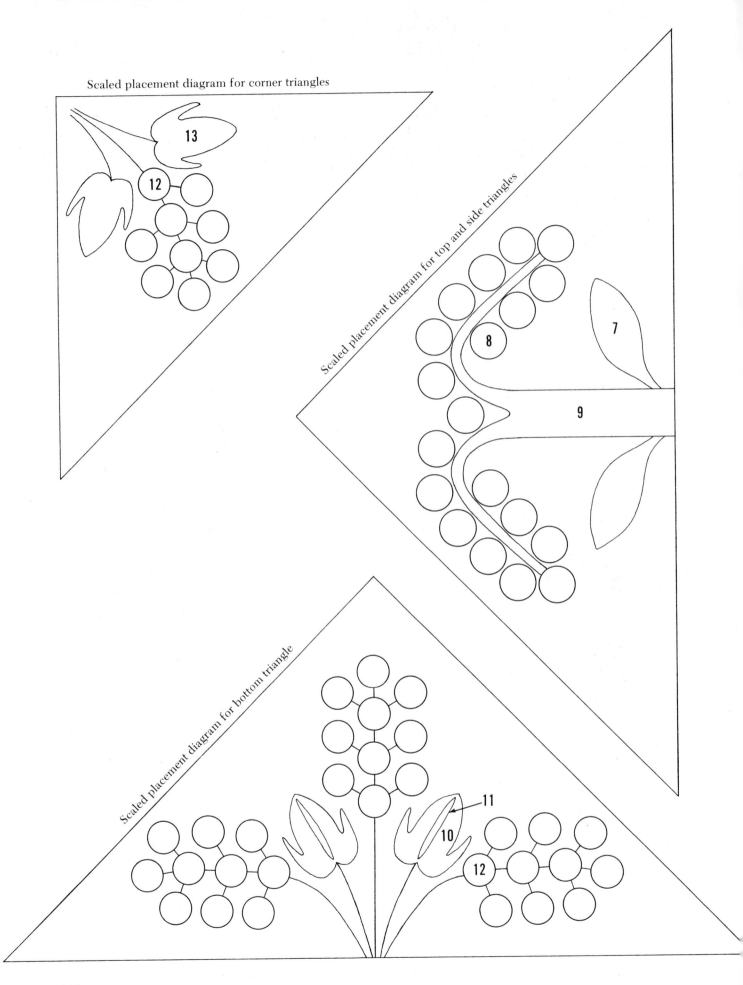

Scaled placement diagram for corner triangles

Scaled placement diagram for top and side triangles

Scaled placement diagram for bottom triangle

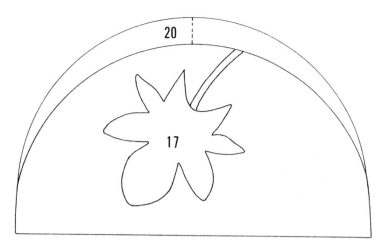

Scaled placement diagram for top scallops

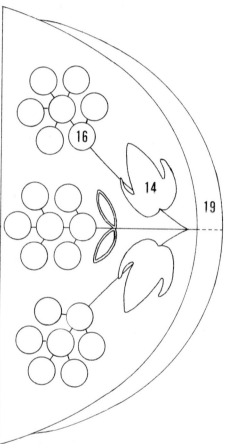

Scaled placement diagram for side scallops

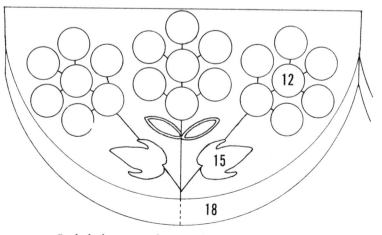

Scaled placement diagram for bottom scallops

243

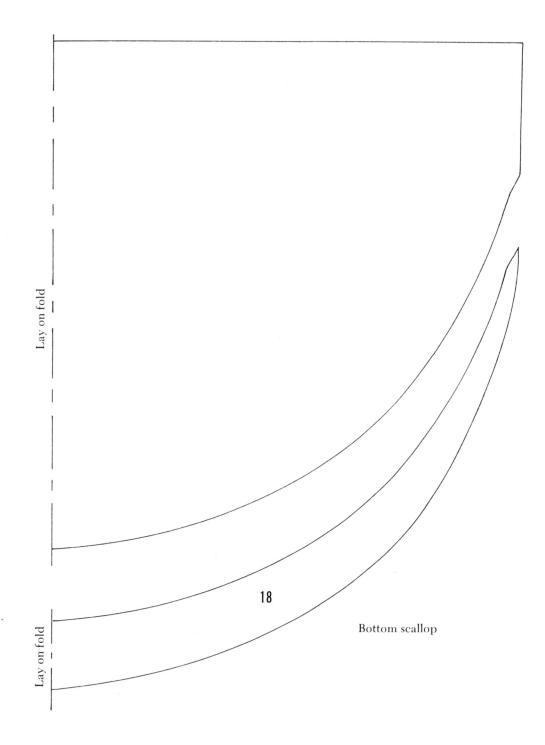

Lay on fold

Lay on fold

18

Bottom scallop

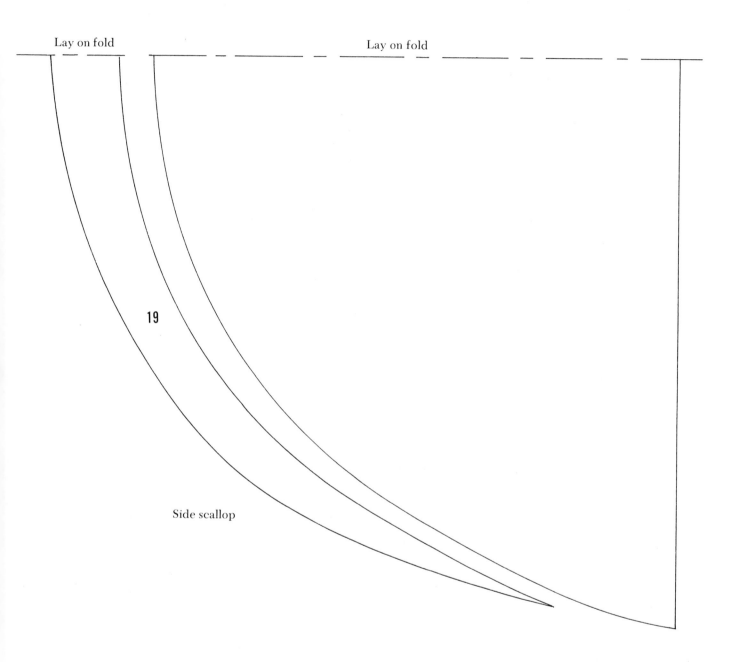

Lay on fold

Lay on fold

19

Side scallop

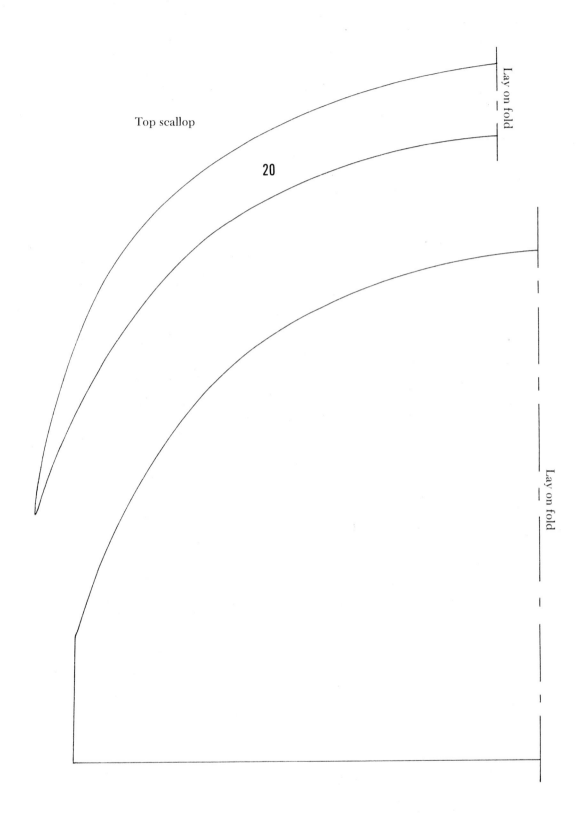

Top scallop

20

Lay on fold

Lay on fold

FEATHERED
WORLD
WITHOUT END

Diagram of quilt illustrated in plate 24

Dimensions: 88 x 71 inches.

Materials: all 45-inch fabrics.

2½ yards brown—includes binding
5 yards gold—includes backing
3½ yards (approximately) scraps in red, white, blue, and assorted dark and medium prints and plaids

Cut: Add ¼-inch seam allowance all around each piece and to each measurement given.

For each motif: (Total of 30 World Without End Stars, 13 inches between points)
1 dark #1
4 medium #2
4 red #3
24 dark or medium #4
32 light #4
4 dark or medium #5 (*see note below*)
4 dark or medium #5, reversed (*see note below*)
4 light #6 (*see note below*)
4 light #6, reversed (*see note below*)

For sets:
49 brown #7
22 brown #8

For borders:
2 gold strips, sides, 3 x 88 inches
2 gold strips, ends, 5 x 65 inches

Directions: Piece each World Without End motif, using the scraps in a variety of color arrangements. Set the motifs together in strips of six, with the brown #7 pieces, then set the strips together and finish the edges with #8 pieces.

Add the side borders, then the end borders. Quilt with Fan or Clamshell design and finish with narrow brown binding.

Note: Pieces #5 and #6 are almost identical to #4, but with very slight shaping to accommodate the curve of #1.

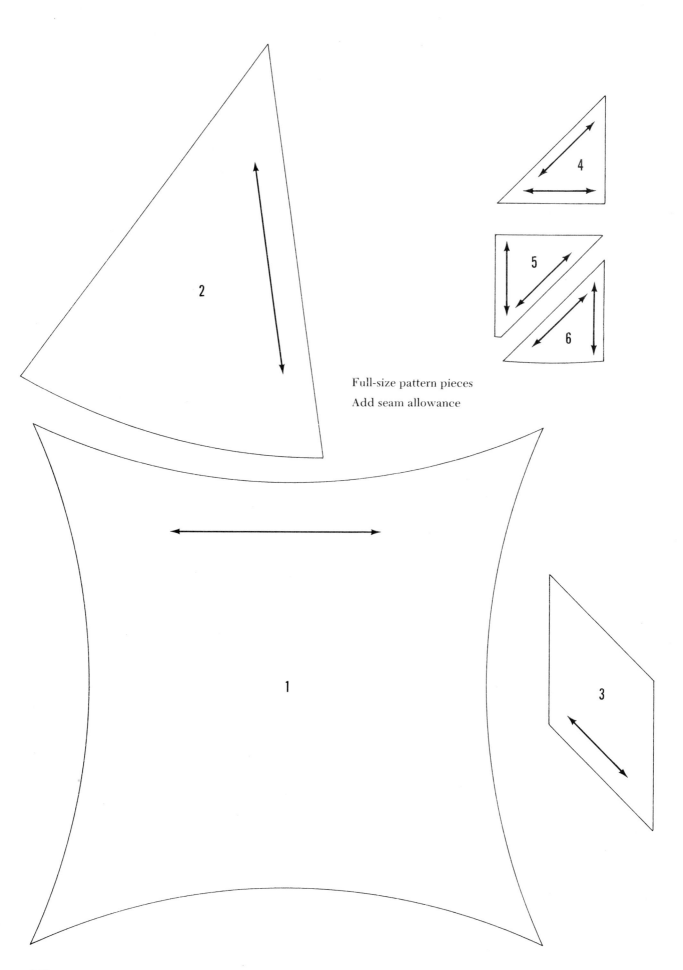

Full-size pattern pieces

Add seam allowance

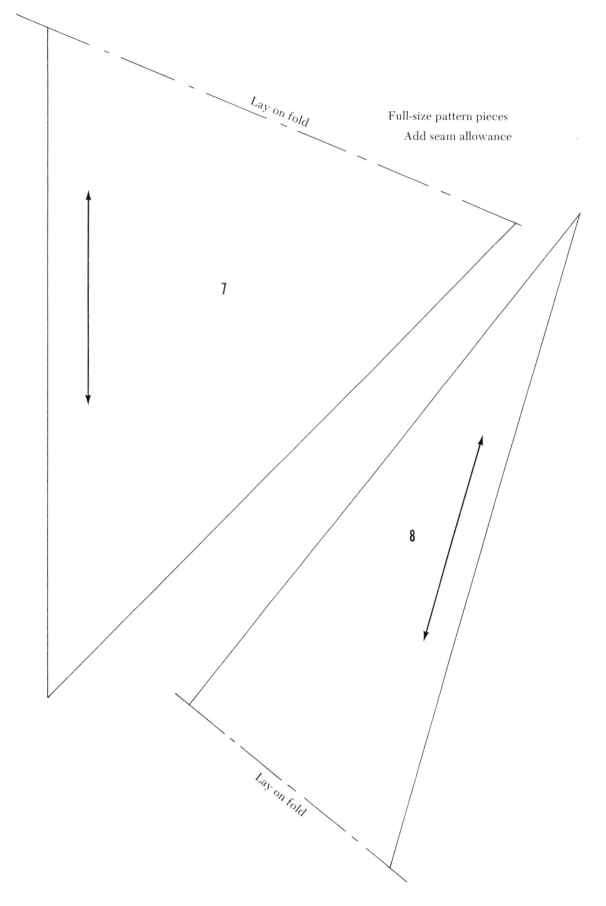

Lay on fold

Full-size pattern pieces

Add seam allowance

7

8

Lay on fold

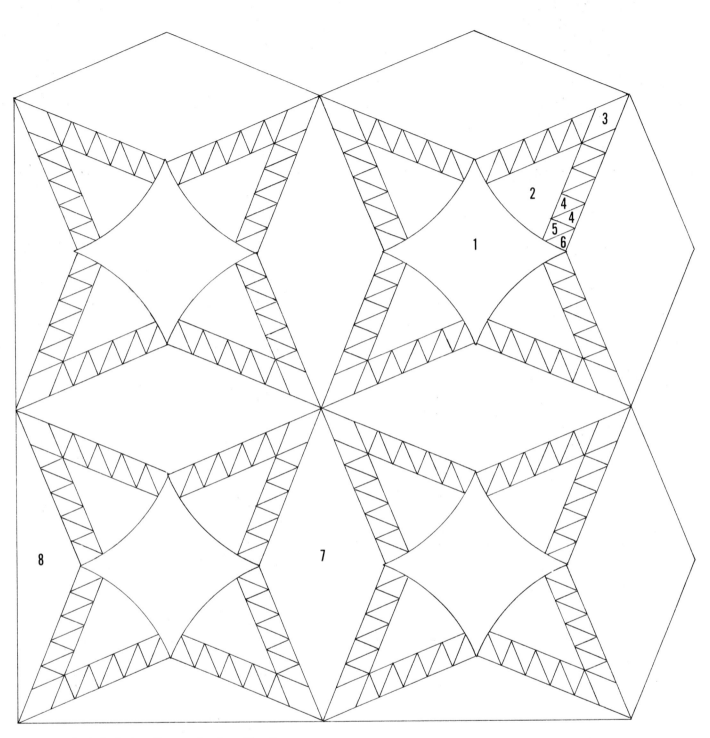

Scaled piecing diagram for 4-motif unit

LADY
OF THE LAKE

Diagram of quilt illustrated in plate 133

Dimensions: 111⅜ x 105 inches.

Materials: all 45-inch fabrics.

2½ yards white
9 yards brown print—includes backing and binding
4 yards (approximately) scraps in browns, pinks, and
   assorted colors

*Cut: Add ¼-inch seam allowance all around each piece
and to each measurement given.*

For each diagonal block: (Total of 153 blocks—9 cut in
   half lengthwise and 8 cut in half crosswise—9 x 9
   inches [approximately], 12⅜ inches on the diagonal)
  1 dark #1
  1 light #1
 16 dark #2
 16 white #2

To complete:
   Pieces for one left-half block to be cut in half
horizontally to form the two corners on the right side.

Directions: Seam the dark and light #1 pieces together.
Piece two strips of three each white and dark #2 pieces
and two strips of five each. Surround the center piece
(the two #1 pieces) with these strips to form the diagonal block.
   Starting at the lower right corner, set the blocks
together in strips, starting and ending with the halved
blocks. The longest strip will have sixteen whole
blocks.
   A small design can be quilted in the center—such as
two concentric circles, a spiral, or a flower—while the
small pieces can be outline quilted. The effect will be
of diagonal crosshatch quilting with the softer rounded
designs in the centers. Finish with very narrow binding
or by bringing the back over to the front as a binding.

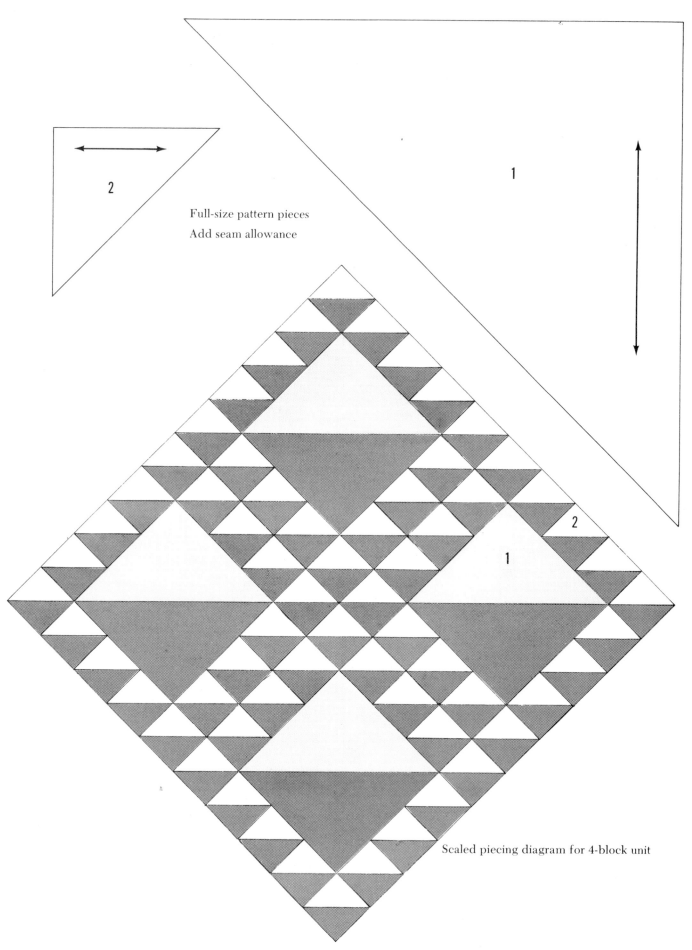

2

1

Full-size pattern pieces
Add seam allowance

2

1

Scaled piecing diagram for 4-block unit

DOUBLE HEARTS

Diagram of quilt illustrated in plate 27

Dimensions: 97 x 97 inches.

Materials: all 45-inch fabrics.

    6 yards white
    8 yards blue and white stripe—includes backing and binding
    5 yards red print—preferably assorted patterns

Cut: Add ¼-inch seam allowance all around each piece and to each measurement given.

For each block: (Total of 18 blocks—4 cut in half and 1 quartered—20 x 20 inches, approximately 28¼ inches on the diagonal)
    1 white square, 20 x 20 inches
    1 red Hawaiian motif

For sashes:
    36 blue strips, 20 x 2 inches
    18 red squares, 2 x 2 inches—6 cut in half for edges

For borders:
    4 blue strips, 93 x 2 inches
    4 red squares, 2 x 2 inches

Directions: Use the Hawaiian appliqué method to place the designs on the blocks. Cut four blocks in half and one in quarters to complete edges.

Set the blocks in diagonal rows with blue sashes. The longest strip will have five whole blocks and will begin and end with a quarter block. Make up the long sashes in the same way, alternating blue sashes and red corner blocks, ending with the halved corner blocks. Join the rows of blocks with the long sashes.

Seam the corner blocks to the ends of two of the borders. Seam the other two borders to two sides of the pieced top. Add the two borders and corner blocks to the other sides. (There is an error in the arrangement of the corner blocks; it seems too obvious to make it necessary to repeat.)

Use outline and echo quilting around the Hawaiian motifs, filling the entire white areas. Quilt the sashes with any small continuous design. Bring the blue backing over to finish the edges.

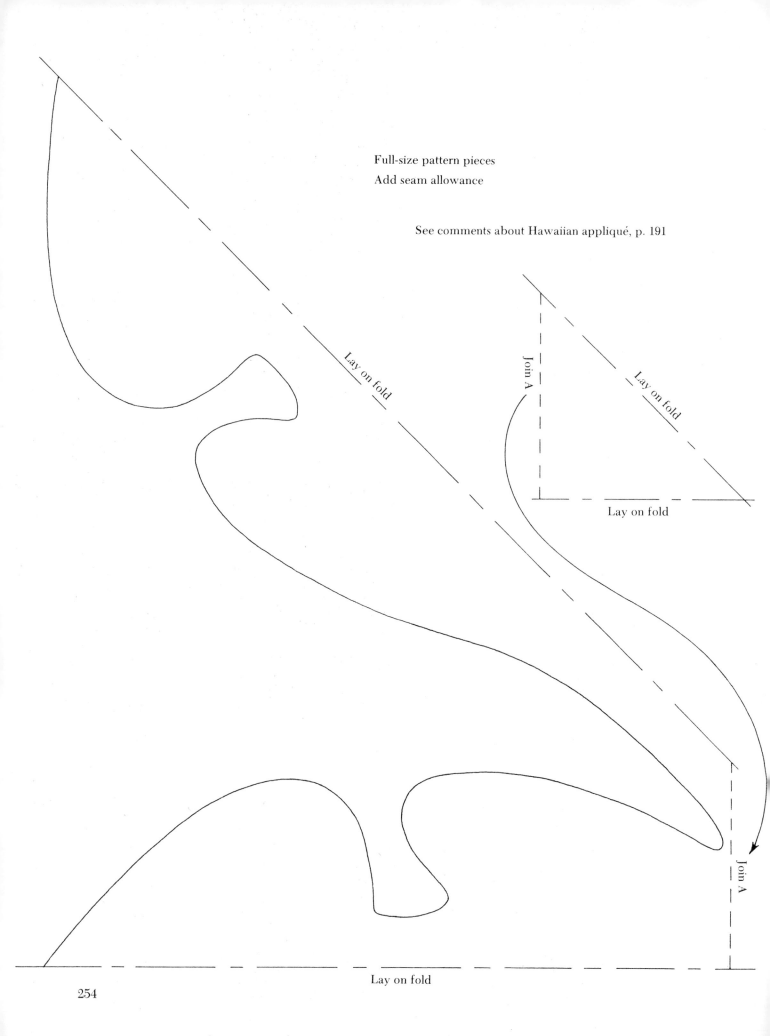

Full-size pattern pieces

Add seam allowance

See comments about Hawaiian appliqué, p. 191

Lay on fold

Lay on fold

Join A

Lay on fold

Lay on fold

Join A

Scaled placement diagram

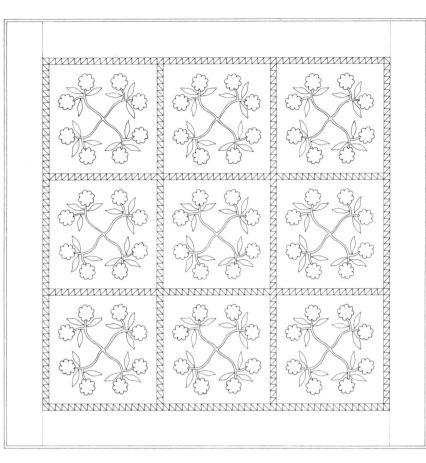

Diagram of quilt illustrated in plate 37

ROSE SPRAY

Dimensions: 89 x 89 inches.

Materials: all 45-inch fabrics.

    6 yards white
    9 yards red—includes backing and binding
    1½ yards green

Cut: Add ¼-inch seam allowance all around each piece and to each measurement given.

For each block: (Total of 9 blocks, 22 x 22 inches)
    1 white square, 22 x 22 inches
    8 red #1
    12 green #2
    4 green #3
    4 strips of green bias, 8 x ⅜ inches, for #4

For sashes and inner borders:
    460 red #5 (*see note below*)
    460 green #5 (*see note below*)

For borders:
    2 white strips, ends, 9 x 71 inches
    2 white strips, sides, 9 x 89 inches

Directions: Appliqué the floral designs to each block. Work the bias stems into graceful curves and group the flowers and leaves evenly in each corner.

Make up six 22-inch sashes from the red and green triangles. Set the blocks together with these in three rows. Make up four long sashes or borders of red and green triangles to join and trim these three rows. Finish the other two edges with strips of red and green triangles. Add white borders at top and bottom and finish with white side borders.

Use outline quilting around the appliqué motifs and diagonal quilting in the background. A Cable or Feather quilting motif can be used in the white borders. Finish the edges with a narrow red binding.

Note: The slightest variation in marking or seaming on the tiny triangles will alter the length of the strips. As long as the effect is even and the lengths correct, the exact number is unimportant.

1

2

3

4

Full-size pattern pieces
Add seam allowance

5

Scaled placement diagram

Sash and border

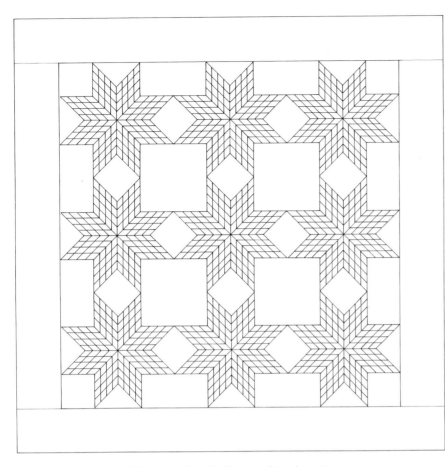

Diagram of quilt illustrated in plate 56

TOUCHING STARS

Dimensions: 108 x 108 inches.

Materials: all 45-inch fabrics.

2½ yards white
6⅛ yards bold paisley print—includes binding
9½ yards yellow print—includes backing
½ to 2 yards print scraps (*see note A below*)

Cut: Add ¼-inch seam allowance all around each piece and to each measurement given.

For each Star: (Total of 9 Stars, 28 inches across—*see note B below*)
8 red diamonds (at the center)
16 dark diamonds (second row)
24 light diamonds (third row)
32 medium diamonds (fourth row)
24 dark diamonds (fifth row)
16 yellow diamonds (sixth row)
8 medium diamonds (at the point)

To complete:
4 white squares, 16½ x 16½ inches
16 white squares, 8¼ x 8¼ inches
8 white rectangles, 16½ x 8¼ inches
12 triangles, 8¼ inches on the right-angle sides

For borders:
2 bold print strips, sides, 84 x 12 inches
2 bold print strips, ends, 108 x 12 inches

Directions: Make up each star point in strips of diamonds, arranging the colors so that each Star has concentric circles of color exploding from the center. Set the Stars together with the necessary squares and fill in the edges with the rectangles and triangles. Four of the small squares will finish the corners. Add side and then end borders.

The four large white squares offer a fine opportunity for show-off quilting. The original has Wreaths worked in these spaces but any gracefully curving design planned for a 16-inch block will do. The remaining spaces and the borders are filled with crosshatch quilting, sometimes set straight and sometimes on the diagonal. Outline quilting should be used in the Stars.

Note A: There may be enough large areas of different colors in the bold print to cut many or all of the shades needed for the star points.

Note B: These colors and numbers of pieces are based on the upper left Star. Each Star will require 128 diamonds, always in multiples of 8 for each color—shades may be varied.

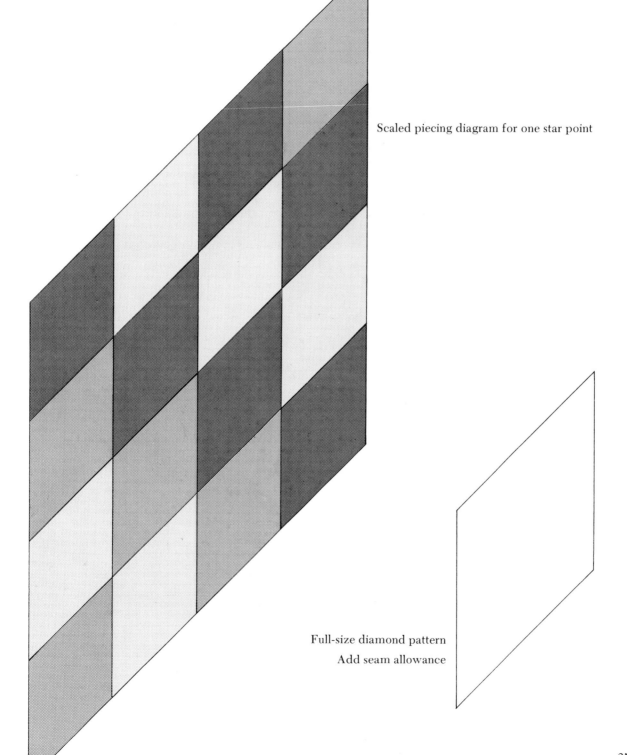

Scaled piecing diagram for one star point

Full-size diamond pattern
Add seam allowance

Diagram of quilt illustrated in plate 94

LOG CABIN IN BARN RAISING VARIATION

Dimensions: 90 x 90 inches.

Materials: all 45-inch fabrics.

  2¾ yards (approximately) dark scraps
  2¾ yards (approximately) light scraps
  8 yards red—includes backing
  1 yard pink for binding (can be used for some light
    scrap also)

*Cut: Add ¼-inch seam allowance all around each piece
and to each measurement given.*

For each block (*see note below*): (Total of 100 blocks,
9 x 9 inches)
  1 red #1
  1 light #2
  2 dark #3-4
  2 light #5-6
  2 dark #7-8
  1 light #9-10
  1 dark #9-10
  2 light #11-12
  2 dark #13-14

  2 light #15-16
  1 dark #17

Directions: Join the strips to the #1 center block in the
following order: clockwise for the first two rows—light
#2, dark #3, dark #4, light #5, light #6, dark #7, dark #8,
light #9. Instead of continuing around, go back and join
dark #10 against dark #8, then continue in a clockwise
direction with light #11, light #12, dark #13, dark #14,
light #15, light #16, dark #17.*

When all of the blocks have been pieced together, lay
them out, turning each block so that the color arrangement matches the one in the picture. Pin and seam the
blocks together in ten strips of ten blocks each. Seam
the strips together, being careful to keep the colors in
the correct order.

Use outline quilting on each piece of each block.
Bind the edge narrowly with pink.

Note: The maker of the original quilt chose some
striped fabrics which add much to the final effect. She
also handled them effectively, even making a change in
the order in which she laid the "logs." With today's
marvelous choice of fabrics it is possible to repeat
much of this artistry.

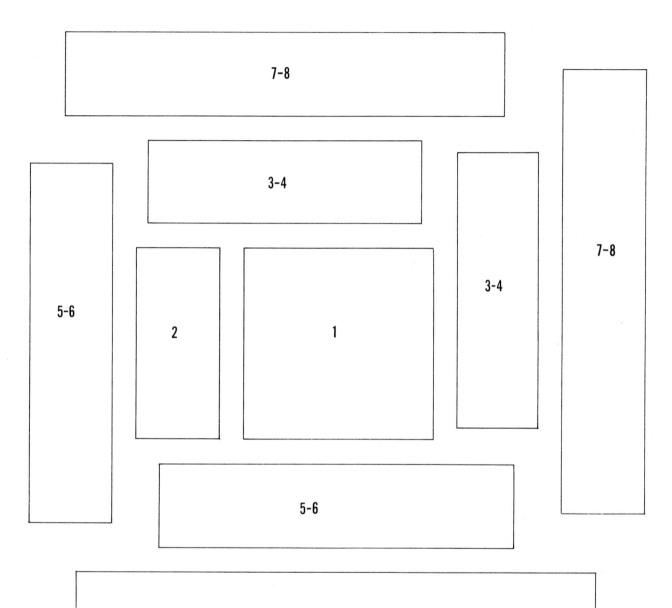

Full-size pattern pieces arranged in order
Add seam allowance

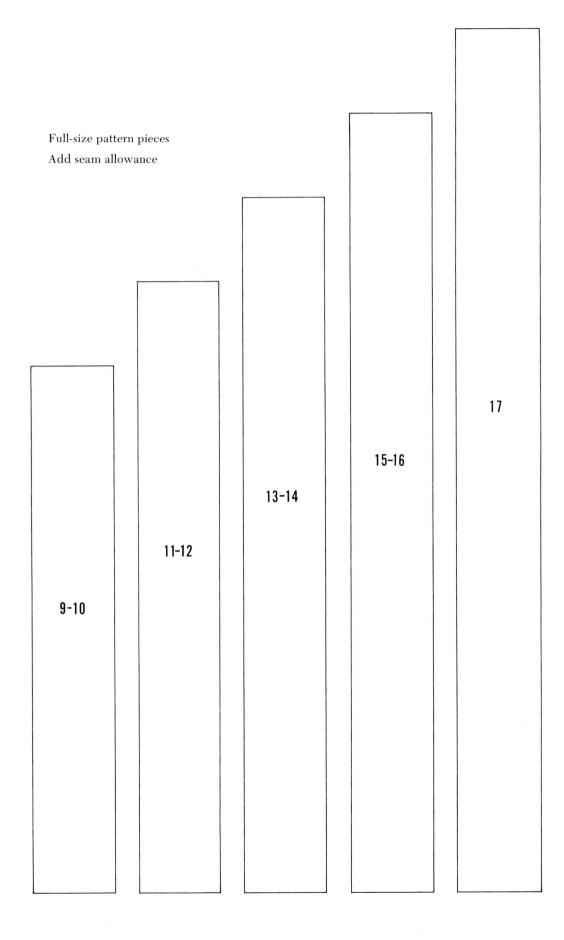

Full-size pattern pieces
Add seam allowance

9-10

11-12

13-14

15-16

17

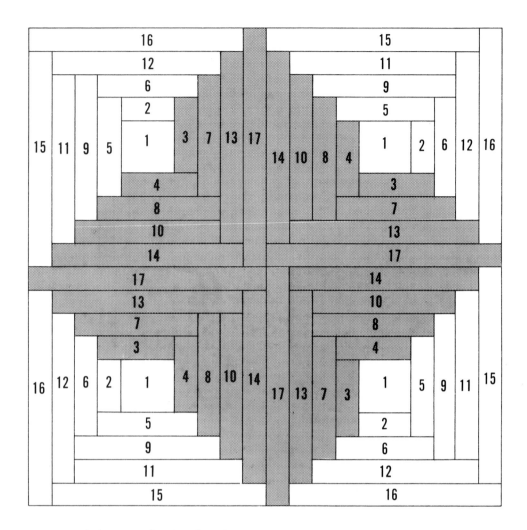

Scaled piecing diagram for 4-block unit

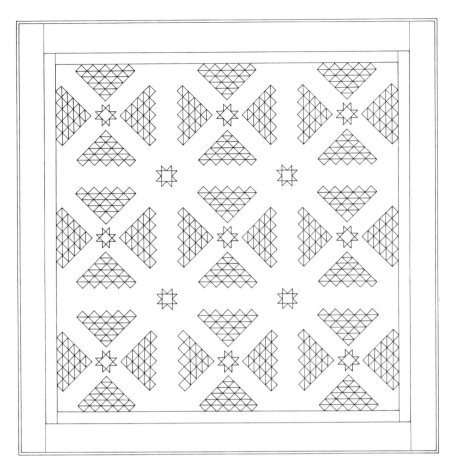

Diagram of quilt illustrated in plate 62

AMISH RAILROAD CROSSING

Dimensions: 84 x 82 inches.

Materials: all 45-inch fabrics.

    4 yards black
    5⅝ yards bright blue—includes binding and backing
    ¼ yard white
    2 yards (approximately) solid-color scraps

Cut: Add ¼-inch seam allowance all around each piece and to each measurement given.

For each block: (Total of 9 blocks, 20 x 20 inches)
    4 black #1
    4 black #2
    1 black #3
    4 black #4
    4 black #5
    8 white #6
  120 bright #7
   24 black #7

For each corner block: (Total of 4 blocks, 4 x 4 inches)
    1 black #3

    4 black #4
    4 black #5
    8 white #6

For sashes:
  12 black strips, 20 x 4 inches

For borders:
    2 blue strips, ends, 68 x 2 inches
    2 blue strips, sides, 72 x 2 inches
    2 black strips, ends, 72 x 6 inches
    2 black strips, sides, 84 x 5 inches

Directions: Piece the four triangles for the sides of each block and the star for the center. Set these together with the black pieces to make nine blocks.

Set the blocks together in rows of three with the sashes, then join the entire center top together with the remaining sashes and corner blocks. Add the blue inner borders and then black outer borders.

The triangle sections can be quilted with outline quilting, but there is room for decorative designs in the sashes and borders. Bind the edge with blue.

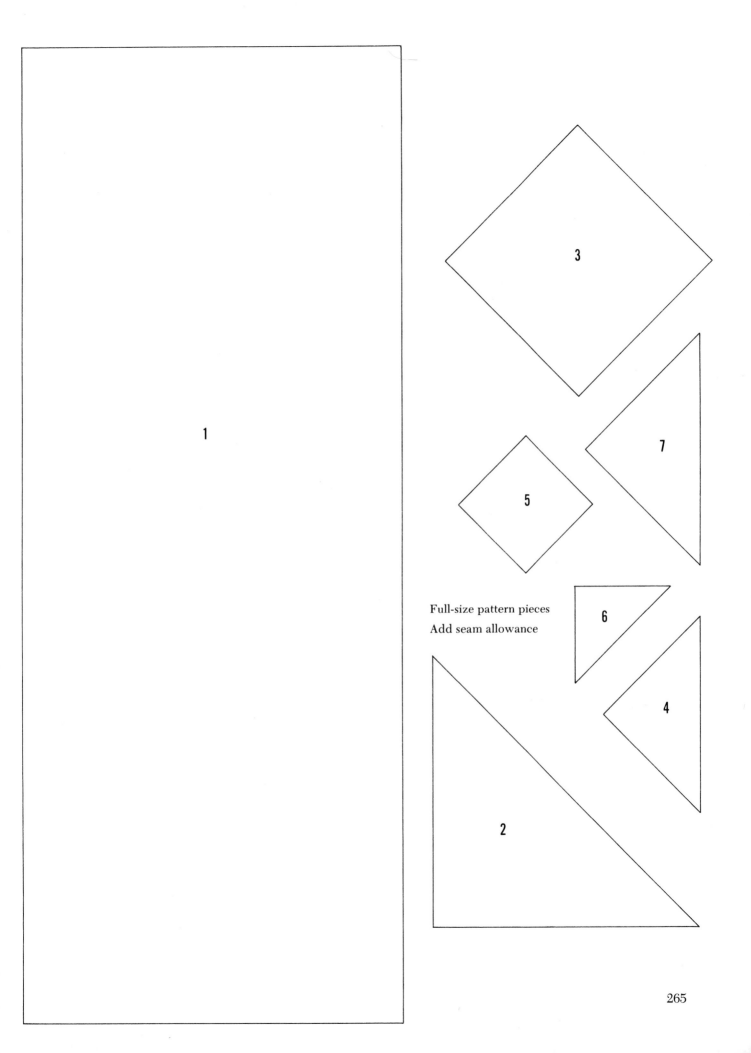

1

3

7

5

6

Full-size pattern pieces
Add seam allowance

4

2

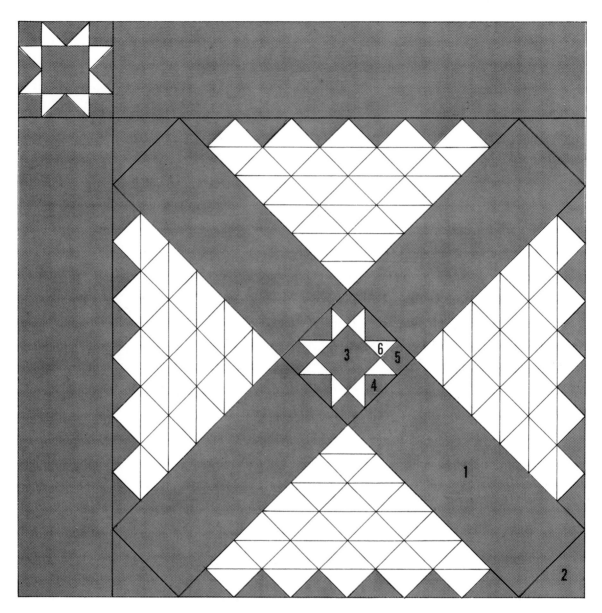

Scaled piecing diagram for block, sashes, and corner block

PIECED TRIANGLES

Diagram of quilt illustrated in plate 135

Dimensions: 92 x 80 inches.

Materials: all 45-inch fabrics.

   1 yard (approximately) light print scraps
   2 yards (approximately) medium print scraps
   3 yards (approximately) dark print scraps
   6½ yards print fabric for backing and binding

Cut: Add ¼-inch seam allowance all around each piece and to each measurement given.

For each block: (Total of 42 complete blocks, 12 x 12
   inches)
   3 light triangles
   6 medium triangles
   9 dark triangles

For each partial block at top: (Total of 6, 12 x 8 inches)
   3 light triangles
   3 medium triangles
   6 dark triangles

For each side border:
  23 medium triangles
  23 dark triangles

Directions: Piece the four squares of each block. Then piece four blocks together to make each unit—nine whole units and three partial units. Piece two long borders to balance the design at the side.

   Use outline quilting all around each piece. Finish the edge with binding from the back.

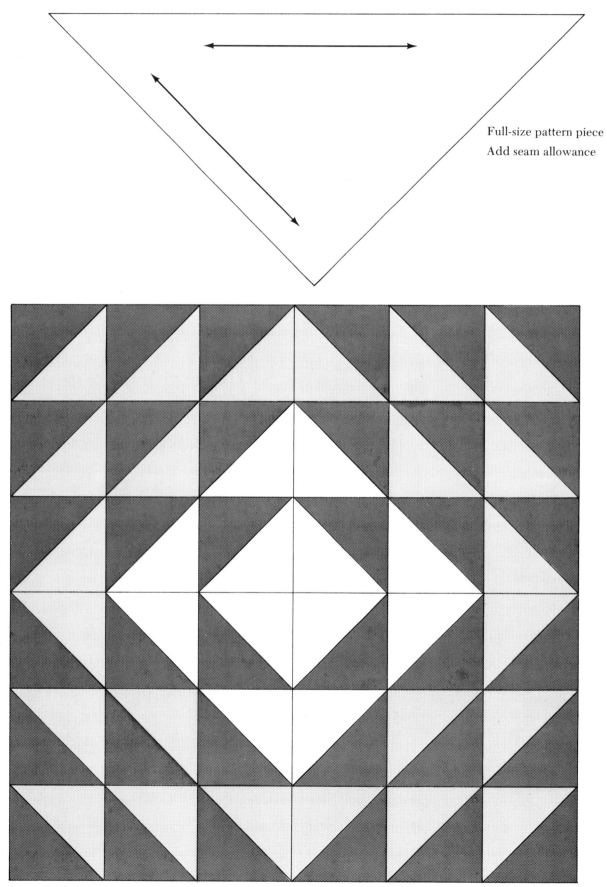

Full-size pattern piece
Add seam allowance

Scaled piecing diagram for 4-block unit

CHIPS
AND
WHETSTONES

Diagram of quilt illustrated in plate 141

Dimensions: 104 x 80 inches.

Materials: all 45-inch fabrics.

9 yards brown print—includes backing and binding
  (1 yard can be in a variety of patterns).
2½ yards white
1½ yards (approximately) blue, pink, other scrap prints

*Cut: Add ¼-inch seam allowance all around each piece
and to each measurement given.*

For each block: (Total of 12 blocks, 20 x 20 inches)
  4 white or light #1
  4 brown #1
  16 medium #1 (mixed, 8 of two colors, or all one color)
  8 white #2
  8 white #3
  4 brown #4

For each sash: (Total of 17 sashes, 20 x 4 inches)
  4 dark #5
  10 white #6
  2 dark #6

For corner blocks:
  6 pink #10

For borders (*see note below*):
  Each end:
  10 dark #7
  22 light #8
  1 dark #8
  2 light #9

  Each side:
  18 dark #7
  34 light #8
  4 light #9

Directions: Piece the round centers and set them into
the frame made with the #4 pieces. Piece the sashes and
set the blocks together in three rows, joined by the
sashes. Make up the two long sashes and the four
borders to complete the top.

  Use outline and echo quilting as heavily as you like,
or use outline on all pieces and small motifs in the
corners of the blocks. Finish the edge with narrow
brown binding.

Note: A slight correction has been made in the number
of pieces in the borders so that they will be even.

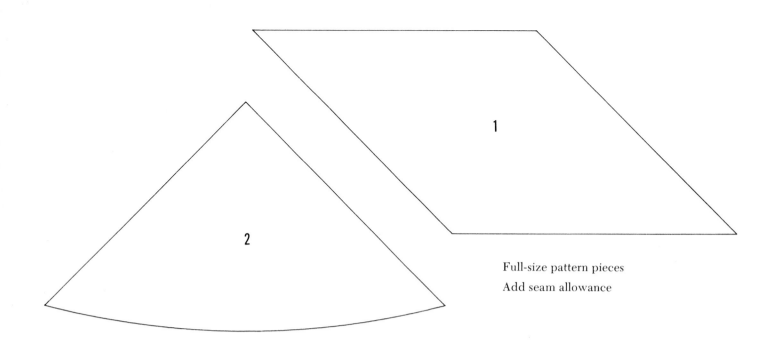

1

2

Full-size pattern pieces

Add seam allowance

Scaled piecing diagram for block, sashes, and corner block

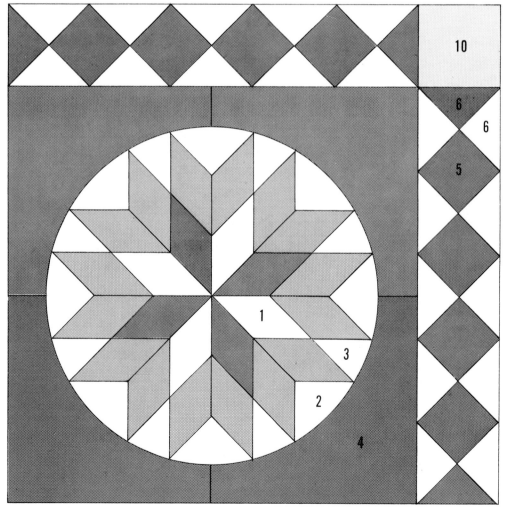

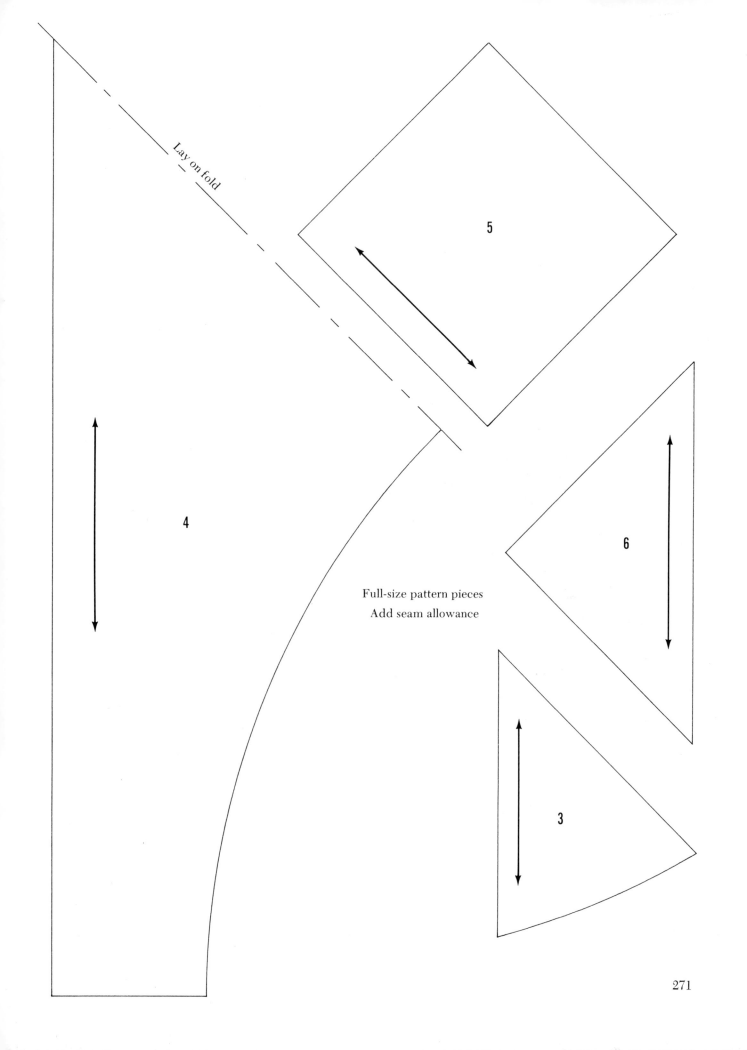

Lay on fold

5

4

6

Full-size pattern pieces
Add seam allowance

3

271

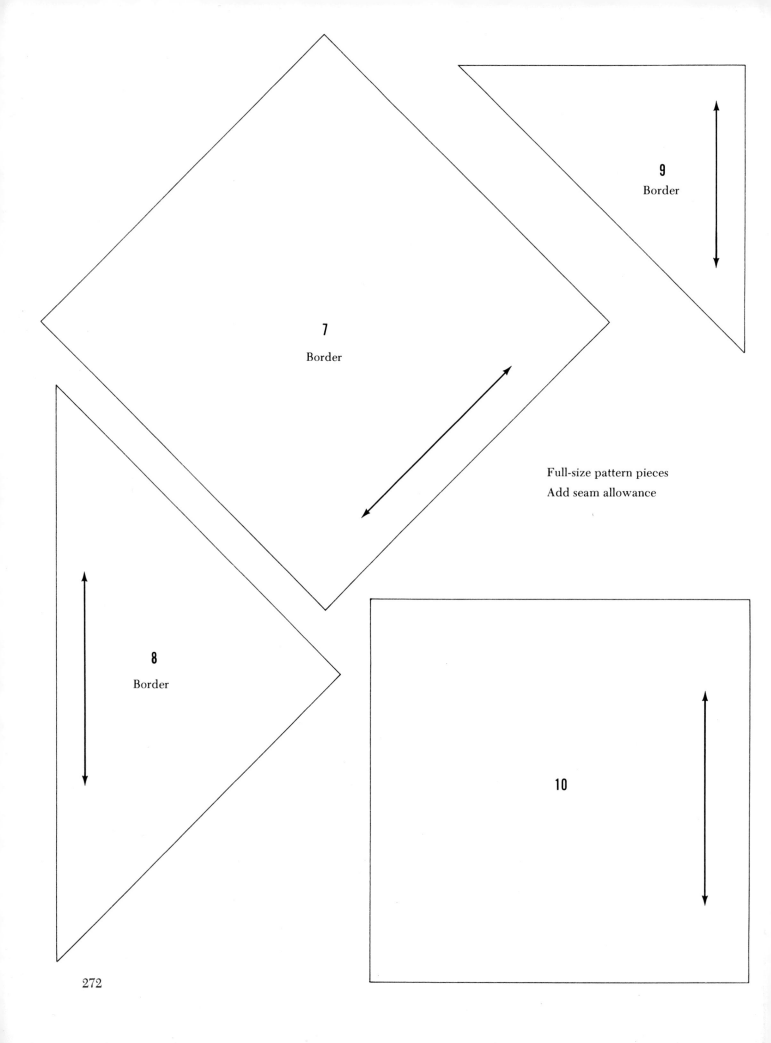

7
Border

9
Border

8
Border

10

Full-size pattern pieces
Add seam allowance